INVITATION TO THE VOYAGE

Pour l'enfant, amoureux de cartes et d'estampes,
L'univers est égal à son vaste appétit,
Ah! que le monde est grand à la clarté des lampes!
Aux yeux du souvenir que le monde est petit!

Baudelaire

TOM HUBBARD was the first librarian of the Scottish Poetry Library, and his last full-time posts, successively in 2011-12, were Distinguished Visiting Professor at the University of Connecticut (Scottish and American literature) and Professeur Invité at the University of Grenoble (Scottish and comparative literature; aesthetics), followed by a writer's residency at Lavigny in Switzerland. He is the author of ten books of fiction, poetry and non-fiction, and editor or co-editor of other works. His most recent books are *The Devil and Michael Scot* (Grace Note, 2020) and *The Emerald Passport: Seumus Heaney, Literature and Europe* (Széchenyi Academy of Literature and Arts, 2022). He is an Irish Scot.

INVITATION TO THE VOYAGE

Scotland, Europe and Literature

TOM HUBBARD

2022

First published 2022
by Rymour Books
with Hog's Back Press
45 Needless Road,
PERTH
PH2 0LE

ISBN 978-1-7395960-0-2

http://www.rymour.co.uk

cover and book design by Ian Spring
printed by Imprint Digital, Exeter, Devon

A CIP record for this book
is available from the British Library

The paper used in this book is approved
by the Forest Stewardship Council

CONTENTS

ACKNOWLEDGEMENTS

I would like to thank Margaret Tejerizo for writing the foreword to this collection and Ian Spring for publishing this book and for his patience throughout the editorial process and for the cover design. These essays have been informed by conversations with friends too numerous to mention and I thank them all. The pieces themselves have appeared mostly in periodicals and composite books or as talks and lectures at various locations. Thanks are due to all those who published or otherwise commissioned them.

'Chosyn Charbukkill' appeared in *La morte di Virgilia: lingua, letteratura, natura, identità*, ed. Elio Cipriani [et al]. Faenza: Edizioni Moby Dick, 1991.

'Henryson's Tragic Fable' was the introduction to *The Flouero Makarheid* [papers on Robert Henryson], ed. Morna Fleming. Dunfermline: The Robert Henryson Society, 2003.

'Scott and *Volkspoesie*', was a paper for a seminar at the Institute of Germanic Studies, University College London, in April 2004.

'Furth of the Isles', was presented at a Reception of British and Irish Authors in Europe (RBIAE) seminar, University College London, December 2002.

'Castle Corbie', *Scottish PEN Blogspot*, 3 December 2011.

'Byron in Love', *Scottish Affairs*, no. 69, Autumn 2009. A review of Edna O'Brien, *Byron in Love*, London: Weidenfeld & Nicolson, 2009.

'Pushkin in Scotland' was a paper for a conference on Pushkin at the University of Glasgow (School of Modern Literatures and Cultures, Russian section), December 2019, subsequently written up for a pamphlet, *Not My Circus, Not My Monkey*, a selection of poems and prose by Sheena Blackhall and Tom Hubbard, Aberdeen: Malfranteaux Concepts, 2020.

'Ivan Turgenev: a Russian in Scotland', *Scottish Review*, 24 August 2021.

'Carlyle, France and Germany in 1870', *Zed2O*, no. 29, Autumn 2005.

'Debut at Antwerp', in *The Flemish-Scottish Connections*, Brussels: Flanders-Scotland Foundation 2002, [1996] the book of the exhibition in the City Hall, Brugge / Bruges, Summer 1996.

'Margaret Oliphant's *A Beleaguered City*', was a faculty lecture to the English Department, Université Stendhal, Grenoble, December 2011.

'Patrick Geddes and the Call of the South', in *The French Connection: Save the Scots College – Montpellier*, ed. Kenny Munro, [Edinburgh:] Save the Scots College Montpellier, with support from the Sir Patrick Geddes Memorial Trust [2013?].

'Revaluation: R.B. Cunninghame Graham', *Cencrastus*, no. 8, Spring

1982.

'Hugh MacDiarmid: The Integrative Vision', *Chapman*, no. 69-70, Autumn, 1992. Originally part of a lecture to MDes students, Glasgow School of Art, summer of 1992, and subsequently published in full in my book *The Integrative Vision: Poetry and the Visual Arts in Baudelaire, Rilke and MacDiarmid*, Kirkcaldy: Akros Publications [Duncan Glen], 1997.

'From Montsou to Bowhill', was a paper presented at a one-day symposium on Joe Corrie at the Byre Theatre, under the auspices of St Andrews University, October 2018.

'The Poetry of George Bruce', *Scottish Review*, 5 May 2021.

'The Indian Summer of Lillias Scott Forbes', *Scottish Review*, 1 September 2021.

'Hamish Henderson as Translator' was written specially for the present book.

'Scandic Scots', in *Minority Languages: The Scandinavian Experience*, ed. Gunilla Blom, Peter Graves, Arne Kruse and Bjarne Thorup Thomsen, Oslo: Nordic Language Secretariat, 1992.

'Scotland and Poland', *Scottish Affairs*, no. 82, Winter 2013. This is a review of T M Devine & David Hesse (ed.) *Scotland and Poland: Historical Encounters, 1500-2010*, Edinburgh: John Donald (Birlinn), 2011.

'Erik Chisholm: A Scot Among the Czechs', *Scottish Review*, 16 June 2021. Based on a seminar paper given at the Masaryk University, Brno in August 2016.

'Doing Something Uncustomary: Edwin Morgan and Attila József' is based on a guest lecture in the Department of Comparative Literature, University of Szeged, on 3rd May, 2006. 'Doing Something Uncustomary', *International Journal of Scottish Literature*, issue one, Autumn 2006.

'Wandering Scots' began life as a guest lecture at the Universities of Mainz and Tübingen, November 1990, and was updated as a paper for the Brussels Branch of the Saltire Society in the Scottish office of the European Union, Brussels, September 1999. It was subsequently published in a Hungarian journal, *Epona*, 2008/2. The present text is an abridged version of the material.

'Writing Scottishly on Non-Scottish Matters', was a paper presented at a conference on 'Homecoming' at Edinburgh Napier University during the summer of 2009.

'Christopher Harvie's *Dalriada*' was written specially for the present book.

The Appendix was based originally on Facebook postings but is presented here in full.

The Postscript is an abridgement of 'From House of Usher to Calton Creek', *Scottish Review*, 8th June 2022.

Tom Hubbard, 2022

FOREWORD

The reader who embarks on this ambitious literary voyage will not be left in any way disappointed by any aspect of the journey! Indeed, from the very point of departure of its beautiful cover, this work opens out a wealth of information about Scotland's literary world, Scottish cultural and linguistic connections and engagements with important European literary figures, including Pushkin and Turgenev – and many others – and all this is presented in the elegant and witty style which characterises the writings of Tom Hubbard.

This is not a rapid journey along a set and well-trodden route which can be undertaken at top speed; the reader will wish to linger and ponder over the fine detail offered and, indeed, in many cases, return again and again to certain places and explore some of the fascinating diversions offered. Within these 150 pages, the reader will encounter a remarkable range of in-depth personal knowledge on the topics, writers and countries dealt with in the book; this, blended with the author's dedication to the subject matter, creates a unique opportunity to make many fascinating discoveries along the way of this literary journey and challenges the reader to re-evaluate and re-visit many aspects of Scottish literature, language and culture.

The book contains twenty-eight sections, each with its own heading and these are preceded by a section entitled 'Ghosts and Flesh – By Way of a Preface'. With a grace and a creative energy, we travel – to give but some examples – from Virgil, Byron, Carlyle, Pablo Neruda. Hugh MacDiarmid, Margaret Oliphant, Robert Louis Stevenson, Carlos Fuentes – and each writer is set in his/her own evocative and memorable setting. Hubbard often adds very pleasing personal touches – such as reminiscences, meetings and home thoughts from foreign journeys of his own.

This is a profound and well-researched collection for the serious scholar of literature who will undoubtedly find many new paths to follow and much information which they will want to investigate further. At the same time, it is a delightful book to savour at one's leisure or, in other words, it can become a slow journey with many stops along the way. Tom Hubbard is always generous with his time and with his creative ideas. Having had the pleasure of collaborating with him during the Centenary Celebrations for Russian at the University of Glasgow in 2017, I recall his inspirational lectures and outstanding contributions. As a trustee of the Scotland-Russia Forum, he continues to share his erudition and innovative ideas, always with that generosity of spirit noted above. It is hoped that this current collection of his essays and articles will be the first journey of many – he certainly has many eager travellers waiting for a new departure.

Margaret Tejerizo 2022

(Formerly Head of Russian, University of Glasgow; Chair of the Scotland-Russia Forum; one of the Editors of *Slavonica*; and currently preparing *The Theatre of Chekhov in Spain: Cries and Whispers*.)

Ghosts and Flesh – By Way of a Preface

'If there is ocht in Scotland that's worth ha'en / There is nae distance to which it's unattached' (Hugh MacDiarmid) The literary traffic between Scotland and its European neighbours, not to mention the rest of the world, has been considerable and ought to be celebrated, but it hasn't been without its blockages, to put it mildly. Back in 1990, Derick Thomson was editing the book that became *Bàrdachd na Roinn-Eòrpa an Gàidhlig*, an anthology of European poetry translated into Gaelic, and published by Gairm. He applied for a publication grant from Glasgow City Council, then presiding over the city's Year of Culture, only to be turned down because of the project's perceived lack of relevance to Glasgow. I was reminded of the Victorian cartoon that showed a top-hatted Mayor of Middle Wallop interrogating a portrait painter in the town's municipal art gallery. 'Oo's that party?' asked the Mayor in front of a likeness of Shakespeare. The artist explained that Shakespeare wrote great plays, was world-famous etc. 'Wot's 'e ever doon for Middle Wallop?' inquired the dignitary. The artist was predictably tongue-tied. 'Well,' the Mayor continued, 'paint 'im out and paint me in.'

'There is a monstrous din of the sterile', wrote MacDiarmid, 'who contribute nothing / To the great end in view'. There are those who complain about the refusal of Gaelic and Scots to crawl away and die, and who consider the promotion of Scottish literature to be nothing but a 'nationalist' plot. The great end continues, with both difficulty and determination, and there's been no little progress since MacDiarmid's day regarding the passage of Scottish culture and into its mainland European counterparts, and vice versa.

It's the vice versa that interests me most. I must say straightaway that I was very heartened during the years I worked on the online Bibliography of Scottish Literature in Translation (BOSLIT) and my research trips to mainland European libraries yielded much in the files of periodicals as well as in books. Some of that work is outlined in the following pages. However, I kept asking myself, OK, they're interested in us; are we interested in them? Well, we were, surely; Derick Thomson's 1990 anthology was an important marker and there were many more examples of the like in Scottish books and magazines. In 1999, the Scottish Poetry Library was awarded an EU grant to purchase books of European poetry in translation as part of its European Poetry Information Centre (EPIC) project.

Scotland can't access EU funds any more. When I worked in Ireland some years back I was amazed to visit a favourite Dublin haunt, Books Upstairs opposite Trinity College, and see shelves of east and east-central European poetry in new versions by Irish poets and published by the Cork-based Southwords Editions. Their list has greatly expanded since then and includes many non-European poets in translation. If only we could have such a set-up in Scotland, I mused, and on such a scale…

Scottish writers, translators and publishers do their heroic best within the limitations. When the veteran Irish poet Pearse Hutchinson (1927-2012) visited Edinburgh in 1992, he proved a great source of morale. Born in Glasgow and retaining his Glasgow accent, he knew what we were about. He was a great linguist and a whole book is devoted to his translations from an array of Latin languages, national and regional. He even has a quatrain from a Galician folk song made into Scots. Of course he has also original poems in Irish, and acts as a conduit between Irish and European languages. The concluding lines of Pearse's 'The Frost is All Over' should resonate with all of us in his native land:

> Are those who rule us, like their eager voters,
> ghosts yearning for flesh? Ghosts are cruel,
> and ghosts of suicides more cruel still.
> To kill a language is to kill one's self.

Chosyn Charbukkill:
Virgil's Northern Legacy

In discussions of the beginnings of modern Russian literature, Dostoyevsky is generally credited with the remark that 'we all came out from under Gogol's overcoat'. All European poetry which is concerned with cultural identity may be said to have come out from under Virgil's mantle. Virgil loved his native land and created an epic for an Italy that might one day become united. Virgil's most celebrated spiritual son, Dante, argued for a vernacular language that would transcend the rivalries of innumerable dialects. By his example -- the *Divina Commedia* he established that language.

In Scotland, the Bishop of Dunkeld, Gavin Douglas, was a passionate patriot at a time of acute political crisis. In 1513 Scotland suffered military defeat on the field of Flodden. Two months previously, the Bishop had completed one of the greatest Renaissance translations, the *Eneados*. Virgil was given to Scotland, and to the world, in the language which Gavin Douglas was the first to call 'Scots'. Prior to this, there had been much confusion over the name of that language. Alas, since Douglas's masterpiece there has been even more confusion over the very language itself, and its survival.

Virgil was prone to doubts that would not be unfamiliar to his spiritual descendants of today. He often felt that he must be crazy to attempt a work on the scale of the *Aeneid*. He did not even live to complete it. Yet how different would have been the course of literary history had he not made that leap of faith. Nor was Gavin Douglas discouraged by any impending disaster for Scotland, nor indeed by Virgil's death. He translated not twelve, but thirteen books of the *Aeneid*. He tells us of his strange dream in which he received a visitor. This was Maffeo Veggio, who had provided the thirteenth book which had been left unwritten by Virgil himself. Maffeo pressed Douglas to undertake the Scots version of Book XIII, arguing with him and beating him with a club. Douglas dared not refuse.

Ezra Pound claimed that Douglas's *Aeneid* is actually superior to Virgil's, because Douglas 'had heard the sea'. Whether or not you agree with that, Douglas has certainly taken a southern poem and turned it into a northern one:

> Reveris ran reid on spait with watteir broune,
> And burnis hurlis all thair bankis downe...

> On raggit rolkis of hard harsk quhyne-stane,
> With frosyne frontis cauld clynty clewis schane...

> Goustly schaddois of eild and grisly deid,
> Thik drumly scuggis dirknit so the hevyne...

> Scharp soppis of sleit, and of the snypand snawe.

I can assure you that Scottish winters can be just like that. Much of Douglas's Virgil has the harsh grandeur of the Scottish landscape, even in the evocations of the Underworld. I hope that does not put anyone off visiting Scotland – it has its brighter, cheerful side! Yet last March I was in the company of Gian Piero Bona, a poet from Torino (Turin); we were visiting a ruined castle north of Glasgow and to get there we had to walk through a rather bleak wood. For Gian Piero in Scotland, 'il vento negli alberi' was actually a source of delight. I explained the Scots word 'eldritch' to him – it means 'weird, ghostly, strange, unearthly'. *Eldritchissimo!*

There are subtle ways in which Douglas shows a very deep affinity with his original. If you turn to the opening of Book I, and compare the Douglas and the Dryden translations, you may notice that Douglas soon uses various forms of the word 'Italy' Almost sixty lines pass before Dryden writes that word. It is as if Douglas the Scottish patriot can identity with Virgil's Italian patriotism. It doesn't seem to be so important to the Englishman. Dryden's version is in the high-flown, sophisticated style of the Restoration period. Douglas's Scots is rugged, earthy, of the people.

That last point is crucial. Today, the Scots language survives among the lower classes. In the *De Vulgari Eloquentia*, Dante asserts that 'our illustrious language wanders about like a wayfarer, and is welcomed in humble shelters, seeing we have no court'. In Douglas's time Scots was the language of the court as well as of the commoners. It had official status. The increasing dominance of England, culminating in the Act of Union of 1707, destroyed all that.

The church and the intelligentsia assisted in the betrayal of the language and it culture In social terms, Scots was driven underground. As it became the speech mainly of the lower classes, it was despised: people beggar to believe that Scots had never been a language and was simply a vulgar, debased form of English. It had also fragmented into dialects. Could this not threaten the concept of Scotland as a diverse but still unified entity? There isn't an easy answer to that question.

Other 'unofficial' languages have been suppressed and have survived. Why has Scots fared less well than them? Much depends on the nature of the suppression. If the dominating culture uses brute force, the suppressed culture becomes all the more determined to survive. Bismarck had Polish schoolchildren beaten for using their language. Poland itself did not exist on the map for a hundred years, but the Polish people refused to allow the language to die. In Spain, the Franco régime banned Catalan and Gallego. Since the dictator's death in 1975, these cultures have reasserted themselves, and there is a measure of home rule from Madrid. In Scotland in 1990 we still have no political autonomy from Westminster; as for the Scots language. It is an object of ridicule by the *litermafiosati* of metropolitan Scotland. If you ridicule a culture and cause reality to be confused with a caricature, you will have a better chance of destroying that culture than by using the cruder methods of more totalitarian and authoritarian régimes.

Yet reports of the death of 'minority', 'unofficial' language-cultures can be greatly exaggerated. You think you hear the last gasps, then suddenly they become the lusty squall of new birth. Pessimism can be too tempting: what chance is there for local recipes from cooks all over Europe when we'll be able to buy a Big Mac hamburger everywhere between Reykjavik and Heraklion, Lisbon and Murmansk? Yet it is when people get bored by materialistic uniformity that they rediscover what is unique in their home cultures. I am currently editing an anthology of contemporary poetry in Scots for the Mercat Press, an Edinburgh-based publisher. Most of the contributions have come from poets under the age of fifty. In the 1990s intelligent young Scots are more nationalistic (with a small 'n') than they were before (in the 1960s, for example, 'Scottishness' was considered uncool). It may still be crazy to write in Scots but it is gradually becoming a saner form of craziness. Finally, let's look at one of these earlier rebirths. All of us writing in Scots owe an intense debt to Hugh MacDiarmid (1892-1978), arguably the greatest Scottish poet of the twentieth century, whose Scots masterpiece is the long poem 'A Drunk Man Looks at the Thistle' (1926). MacDiarmid considered that the Scots language yielded a 'Dostoyevskian débris of ideas'; as it had been driven underground it could express much that was subterranean in Scottish thought and feeling – or, in Jungian terms, our collective unconscious. Virgil, Dante, Dostoyevsky – they all descended into subterranean regions – Hell? or Mother Earth in labour? Dostoyevsky gave us the Underground Man. MacDiarmid gave us the Drunk Man looking at the Thistle - Scotland's national emblem. In his book *Hugh MacDiarmid and the Russians* (1987), Peter McCarey suggests that Dostoyevsky's relationship to the Drunk Man is analogous to Virgil's relationship to Dante – the historical personage becomes mystical, and is the guide and mentor to one who voyages through darkness. Dostoyevsky saw a messianic role for Russia, as saviour of Europe. For MacDiarmid's Drunk Man, Scotland, too, is the 'stane that the builders rejec', which 'becomes the corner-stane'.

Can these inebriated nocturnal visions survive and even flourish in daylight sobriety? 1992 is supposed to be the year of super-Europe: it also marks the centenary of Hugh MacDiarmid's birth. In that year the Scottish Poetry Library intends to hold an international festival devoted to poetry in Europe's lesser-used languages. If all goes well we hope to celebrate such riches in the theatres, galleries, cafés and howffs of the Old Town of Edinburgh. That part of the city has a subterranean, labyrinthine atmosphere: I like to think that the shade of Virgil will be moving among us.

NOTE: *Chosyn charbukkill*, part of Gavin Douglas's praise of Virgil, in the Prologue to Book 1 of the *Eneados*. 'The carbuncle was said to shine in the dark. Precious stones were commonly employed symbols of excellence' (A M Kinghorn, ed., *The Middle Scots Poets*, 1970).

SUPPLEMENTARY NOTE: Over thirty years on, this piece must read somewhat quaintly. Moreover, my sentence 'Dostoyevsky saw a messianic role for Russia, as saviour of Europe' now sounds sinister.

Henryson's Tragic Fable
(Introduction to the book *The Flouer o Makarheid*)

Matthew McDiarmid claimed that *The Testament of Cresseid* was the greatest tragic poem between Dante and Shakespeare. Considered solely within Scottish literary tradition, that work could be regarded as a major source of myth and archetype, almost as if – like Gogol's *The Overcoat* in Russia – it created (or at least partly created) that very tradition.

Edwin Muir, who wrote a key essay on Henryson, distinguished between the story, the contingencies of our everyday material lives, and the fable, that spiritual dimension which we might variously call God or poetry, and which we perceive in moments of illumination that break through our quotidian preoccupations. A great poem is one which we feel to be part of a greater, unwritten poem: it is not surprising, therefore, that later poets have been moved to explore the implications within and beyond the corpus of Henryson's work. In a sense they are following Henryson's own example in retelling or amplifying motifs in Aesop and Chaucer. The Henryson revival in Dunfermline itself, over the past ten years, has been marked by an instinctive recognition of such creative ecology. Indeed, there has been a transference from verbal to visual forms, as apparent in the iron gates, by the Abbot House, which carry figures of animals from Henryson's Aesop; in Virginia Colley's murals, enhancing the Abbot House's Presence Room, and depicting scenes from *The Testament of Cresseid*, and in the schools art competition, organised by the Robert Henryson Society

In what follows, Graham Caie offers us a fascinating take on the dialectic of tradition and the individual talent. Writing as the late middle ages became poised toward the Renaissance, Henryson is indeed recycling, but recycling in his own original way. The poet's status approaches that of a named bourgeois individual – by analogy, as it were, with Muir's claim that a Shakespeare character is more assertively unique than Henryson's resigned, accepting (and thus very medieval) Cresseid. Kevin McGinley's comparison of Boethius and Henryson perceptively reveals the tension between the poet's deference to the master philosopher and his insistence that philosophy won't keep disease and hunger at bay; it's as if the smelly, sweaty story is reclaiming its imperfect humanity from the sometimes aloof, antiseptic fable. Henryson is a warm, laconic Fifer with a wary attitude to fine talk, but who knows that fine talk has its place. As McGinley points out, the pun on 'pietie' establishes a link between pity and piety. Behind the faux-naif persona there is a subtle, shrewd wit in collaborative equipoise with the compassion.

Sarah Dunnigan's study also turns on the perennial quivering between the piety and the pity, but within a richly detailed context of female archetypes. Cresseid, inhabiting a no-man's-land (but perhaps some-women's-land) between sinner and saint, is 'love's martyr'. Dunnigan is good, too, on Cresseid's *stigmata*-as-leprosy. The disease, including those afflictions for which it is a scarcely-euphemistic metaphor, has struck deep into the grimmest recesses of the Scottish consciousness. Among places still on the map, Aberdeen's spital and Inverkeithing's lazaretto sound as chilling as ever; AIDS hasn't gone away, of course, and old or new diseases are variously revived or introduced as billions are spent on wars. The physical squalor of leprosy, as the objective-correlative of moral-social decay, was to re-emerge in Scottish literature in the work of our late-Victorian equivocator, Robert Louis Stevenson: turn to his essay on Father Damien, and to the blotches on the skin of Keawe, that devil's lottery-winner in *The Bottle Imp*.

Nick Haydock interrogates the nature of Henrysonian tragedy, and in so doing he challenges us to consider the nature of tragedy generally. Aristotle and his Arab interpreter, Averroës, were core influences on the Scottish polymath Michael Scot (c1175–c1235), but Haydock warns us to distinguish between the two. He proceeds with a subtle analysis of Averroës's divergence from his Greek mentor as regards tragic theory, and demonstrates how the former can illuminate Henryson's moral universe in *The Testament of Cresseid*. I commend Haydock's situation of Henryson's poem within the wider matter of Troy, in particular the death of Cresseid as part of the chain of events leading to the city's fall. We might further consider his claim that the Henryson *oeuvre* forms an integrated whole. In effect, this is a demonstration of how the micropoetics expand into the macropoetic, the individual stories into the overall 'fable' (comic and tragic).

Dunfermline is forever twinned with Troy, by means of Cresseid, and indeed with several points in between: Henryson's greatest poem has travelled much into other languages – see the records of BOSLIT (the online Bibliography of Scottish Literature in Translation) which I edit from the National Library of Scotland. It was something of an epiphany, in July 2002, to hear talks on Henryson delivered at the conference centre of Rolduc, a few minutes' walk from the Dutch-German border.

> The withered floor o lipperheid steps oot
> Tae pick hir road in rags thru foreign warlds
>   (William Hershaw, 'Cresseid – an Allegory')

Henryson himself appears to have crossed frontiers, to have been a 'wandering Scot', equally at home in a Sorbonne lecture-ball and in the classroom of a Fife dominie. His legacy has infinite locations and reverberations.

Scott and *Volkspoesie* in the Borders

In discussing Scotland's *Volkspoesie* – indeed its *Grenzpoesie* – one addresses oneself primarily to poetry with a strong narrative thrust – ballads – and here I have to declare an interest.

I write ballads – in Scots – based on folktales; my poetry pamphlet *Scottish Faust: poems and ballads of eldritch lore* was published by a small press, James Robertson's Kettillonia, earlier this month. As a literary writer I tweak the stories according to the vagaries of my own imagination – but then that's what goes on within the oral tradition. Oral transmission means that the material is in constant flux. Put it another way: we're talking of a poetry that's subject to much metamorphosis, a fluid poetry that belongs to the domain of singers rather than to a corpus of fixed texts to be picked over by academics.

Granted, my ballads are the product of someone who is an academic, or at least a para-academic, and on the verso of the title-page you'll see © Tom Hubbard 2004. The notion of intellectual property is taken as a given in our (relatively) highly literate and individualistic culture.

Also, I've written them, not sung them. Go into certain pubs in Edinburgh, and speak to my folksinger friends; they'll tell you that a ballad isn't fully a ballad until it's sung. So, until these poems jump from the page into performance, I'm a fraud.

The word *ballad* is etymologically related to the word *ballet*. This underlines the notion of the ballad as a natural *Gesamtkunstwerk*: it's created to be sung and danced as well as to be a verbal construct. Ezra Pound declared, in his *ABC of Reading*, that when music gets too far from dance, it's in trouble, and when poetry gets too far from music, it's in trouble.

The vogue for ballad poetry throughout Europe in the late eighteenth and early nineteenth centuries is in large part a reaction against the perceived effeteness, the anaemia of neoclassicism. Step forward the savage, noble or otherwise, with his native woodnotes wild.

Step forward also Johann Gottfried von Herder, who believed in the *uniqueness* of each country's literature, having regard to its very particular social, cultural and economic contexts. Herder saw European literature, by the late eighteenth century, as afflicted by stuffiness, artificiality, abstraction; he questioned the inhibiting effect of bland neoclassical models that had been assumed to possess universal primacy. He proposed that Europe could learn from its relatively uncultivated margins, such as Scotland. (Actually, for centuries Scotland had been one of the most highly sophisticated and cultured countries in Europe ...)

Anyway, the already-existing German love of Scottish folk song and ballad was reinforced by Herder. This existing interest had been nurtured by Bishop Thomas Percy's *Reliques of Ancient English Poetry*, published in 1765. Herder also translated Robert Burns; his version of Burns's lyric 'John Anderson my Jo' goes by the rather boring title of 'Die goldne Hochzeit'. Burns's impact on continental Europe is huge. So also is that of the anonymous folk poetry from which Burns derives: the Scottish ballads were translated into many European languages from the late eighteenth century onward. Herder himself translated Scottish border ballads such as 'Edward, Edward', which is the most eerily dramatic piece collected by Percy.

German translations of the ballads are actually legion, but I would single out as a follow-up to Herder the appearance in Heidelberg, in 1813, of a slim volume called *Drei altschottische Lieder* compiled by Wilhelm of the brothers Grimm: the three 'Lieder' in question are actually ballads, printed in Grimm's German versions, facing the original texts.

Beethoven and Haydn, no less, produced settings of Burns and Scottish folk songs. I'm sorry to have to tell you that their Edinburgh publisher, George Thomson, was rather slow to pay them their fee – a particularly serious matter in Beethoven's case – so there's at least one Scottish stereotype all too sadly confirmed. (The case of Ossian in German-speaking Europe is a vast subject in itself – you may follow it up in the volume of essays on the reception of Ossian, published in the Reception of British and Irish Authors in Europe (RBIAE) series, and edited by my Edinburgh University colleague Howard Gaskill.)

How, then, does Walter Scott fit into all this? He came from the region of the ballads, the Borders. He went to school in Kelso, just a few miles from the English frontier, and where, a few weeks ago, I gave a talk on Vienna 1900. This was to the Kelso Arts and Appreciation Society. We do well not to underestimate the rich cultural life, over the centuries, of the Scottish Borders region.

With such a cultural pedigree, it was fitting that Scott would make his first international mark with the *German*-speaking world. In 1799, aged 28, he translated Goethe's drama *Götz von Berlichingen*, the tale of a chivalrous mediaeval German knight. This was the point of departure for Scott's own creative work, for his series of narrative poems, historical novels, and mediaeval pastiche-romances. (I'm not using the word pastiche in any derogatory way.)

Three years before his version of *Götz*, right at the start of his literary career, Scott had made his own versions of German ballads, notably Bürger's 'Lenore'. To go even further back, these German ballads had taken their cue from the border ballads of England and Scotland – ie, from those collected by Bishop Percy. Exactly a hundred years ago, in the *Modern Language Quarterly* of 1904, E I M Boyd published a very detailed account of the influence of Percy's *Reliques* on German literature.

So it all amounts to a vigorous to-ing and fro-ing of cultural traffic between Scotland and Germany – a true dialogue, and a sustained one at that. Scottish writers have continued to translate German-language writers. Carlyle's contribution in this respect is integral to his œuvre as a whole. Edwin and Willa Muir, notably, introduced Kafka and Hermann Broch to the English-speaking world. Less well-known is Sir Alexander Gray, who made Scots versions of German, Danish and Dutch ballads, as well as of short poems by Heine. More recently, Scottish poets have made versions of Austrian and germanophone Swiss poetry.

We return to Scott and the nineteenth century. There was a need for a new ballad collection that could keep up the momentum of Percy, a collection that would be a more authentic gathering of folk poetry than Percy has provided.

After all, many of the pieces in Percy's *Reliques of Ancient Poetry* are not all that ancient, nor particularly Scottish! Percy includes Drayton, Daniel, Jonson, Suckling, Lovelace – and even Dryden, as 'ancient' poets, in 1765. Walter Scott, however, grew up in border country, in ballad country. Like all frontier territories, it yielded fictional narratives representing extremes of love and death, or, if you prefer, sex and violence. Scott's anthology, *The Minstrelsy of the Scottish Border*, was published first in Kelso in 1802, then an expanded three-volume edition appeared in Edinburgh during 1803. This was the first work by Scott to exert an influence on mainland Europe and my research has identified a large number of translations, into various languages, of the ballads printed by Scott.

The music critic and Wagner expert Ernest Newman, warning against confusing the content of a work of art with the life of the artist, remarked that just because there's pepper in the soup doesn't mean that there's pepper in the cook. For all the passion and excitement of the border ballads, Scott himself was the sober Edinburgh lawyer, a Tory unionist, someone who accepted the humdrum bourgeois realities of the nineteenth century even as he wrote of border raids, ladies on lakes, medieval knights and leaders of Highland clans. He was hard-headed; not, however, hard-hearted. There was much in Scott that regretted the passing of the old ways. Take the key scenes, in *Rob Roy*, between the eponymous Rob, the declining feudal Highland chieftain and outlaw, and his cousin Baillie Nicol Jarvie, the up-and-coming stolid Glasgow merchant. Scott's sympathies are seriously divided, hence the power of these scenes.

Now this tension between the nostalgically romantic and the resignedly realistic animates his compilation of *The Minstrelsy of the Scottish Border*.

By such efforts I may contribute somewhat to the history of my native country; the peculiar features of whose manners and character are daily dissolving into those of her sister and ally. And, trivial as may appear such an offering, to the manes of a kingdom, once proud and independent, I hang it upon her altar with a mixture of feelings, which I shall not attempt to describe.

So, from the very beginning of the nineteenth century, Scott's *Minstrelsy* overtook Percy's *Reliques* as Europe's source of Scottish balladry. That didn't mean that pieces from Percy dropped away; on the contrary, the ballad 'Edward, Edward', already mentioned, became the most translated of the Scottish ballads.

The second most translated ballad, 'Sir Patrick Spens', appears in both the *Minstrelsy* and the *Reliques*. There are German versions of this ballad by Herder and Theodor Fontane. (Fontane is better known as the major German figure of realism in the nineteenth century novel.) The first stanza of the original introduces what is a mini poetic drama – a true performance piece. The scene is set straight away – the king in his tower, and his question put briskly and without any fuss. There's the use of direct speech, the lack of authorial intrusion; there's no indication of 'he said' but we know it's the king speaking. In performance, of course, that can be even clearer. But the point is that this is the ultimate in laconic, all the way to the grim conclusion. All in all, 'Sir Patrick Spens' is a superb example of what W J Entwistle, in his book *European Balladry*, called 'the magic of words unspoken'.

The Scottish ballads may have had an enormous impact on European romanticism, but they lack sentimental romantic gush. There's nothing here akin to the execrable productions of the great charlatan, James Macpherson aka Ossian, upon whose 'songs' of Selma the young Werther drooped so ineffectually. The brutally laconic quality belongs also to that most macabre of ballads, 'The Twa Corbies', which Scott printed in the *Minstrelsy*. Pushkin, who translated it into Russian, revered Scott:

> The chief fascination of Walter Scott's novels lies in the fact that we grow acquainted with the past, not encumbered with the *enflure* of French tragedies, or with the prudery of the novels of sentiment, or with the *dignité* of history, but in a contemporary, homely manner [...] Shakespeare, Goethe, Walter Scott, have no slavish passion for kings and heroes. They don't (as French heroes do) resemble menials mimicking *la dignité et la noblesse*.

There's Pushkin in his customary sardonic mode: one can see how 'The Twa Corbies' would have appealed to him.

Hans Christian Andersen made a Danish version of 'The Twa Corbies', and ten Kate followed this up with a Dutch version based on Andersen's. It's at least arguable that 'The Twa Corbies', composed in a Germanic language – Scots – translates more effectively into other Germanic languages such as Danish and Dutch rather than into a non-Germanic language like Russian. Perhaps this may explain much of the affinity which the Germans felt for the Scottish ballads.

Be that as it may, Andersen's translation of 'The Twa Corbies' appears in his libretto for an opera based on *The Bride of Lammermoor*. With music by the young Danish composer Ivar Bredal, the work was performed in May 1832 and was something of a hit. Andersen was a passionate admirer of Scott, and indeed of Scotland; his tourist trip to our country was one of the high points of his life. He was in his glory in a boat crossing the Firth of Forth, a fiddler

– or rather a violinist (same thing, really) – in attendance as he approached the castle of Ravensheuch (Ravenscraig) featured in Scott's 'Rosabelle'. Andersen wanted his opera to *look* Scottish, complete with kilts and the like trappings, and he explained that the insertion of an authentic Scottish ballad like 'The Twa Corbies' was intended to reinforce the opera's sense of place.

The nineteenth century reception of the Scottish ballads as collected by Percy and Scott raises many fascinating issues that cry out for detailed research, for example: how far were these rough poems domesticated and gentrified for performance in Biedermeier homes? What were the ideological imperatives which impelled translators *outwith* the German-speaking world, sometimes in lands dominated by a Germanic power? *Grenzpoesie* as part of *Grenzpolitik*?

In Bohemia, cultural nationalists, determined to assert the status of the Czech language, discovered the riches of Slavonic folk song and ballad. To raise the status of a language, it helps it if you can create a literature in that language, so the Czechs proceeded from existing Slavonic ballads to their Scottish counterparts, translated them into Czech, and thus added to the store of Czech poetry.

The irony is that while Scotland might have inadvertently advanced the cause of Europe's small nations, that country itself was a small European nation which chose not to become part of the nineteenth-century drive toward independent nationhood. Cultural and political Scottish nationalism did not return as a serious force until well into the twentieth century. But that, as a great English writer once said, is another story.

Furth of the Isles: Walter Scott's Poetry
in Translation During the Nineteenth Century

My proposal is that pre-1900 mainland European response to Scott's poetry implies a cultural phenomenon qualitatively different from that pertaining to interest in his novels.

Common to the reception of the poems and the novels is a cultural-nationalist agenda, but whereas the fiction sets in motion the whole genre of the historical novel, the poetry both draws on the hoard of European balladry and folksong and in turn reanimates that hoard.

That the development of the historical novel takes its cue from Scott, is of course well known, and we regularly invoke the names of Balzac and Tolstoy. The Scott volume in the Routledge Critical Heritage series includes appraisals by Heine, Goethe, Stendhal, Taine as well as by Balzac himself. In the *smaller* language cultures of nineteenth-century Europe, András Thaisz's Hungarian translation of *Ivanhoe*, published in Pest in 1829, was a prelude to the Hungarian historical novel, and one of the greatest critics of Scott and of the historical novel genre is a Hungarian, György Lukács.

However, Scott's poems preceded his novels, and when they reached mainland Europe they were appropriated within an already-existing European genre which I would describe broadly as the ballad/folksong. Ballad and folksong can't easily be divided into two sub-genres for the convenience of literary classifiers – they mesh so much into each other. Thomas Crawford in his influential short book on Scott, first published in 1965 and revised in 1982, considers the long narrative poems to be expanded ballads, with their deployment of such devices as incremental repetition and of the traditional narrative situations of folksong – for example, in *The Lady of the Lake*, where the King of Scotland travels around his realm incognito and falls in love with a commoner, Ellen, whom he encounters in her boat on the loch as he wanders through the Highland forest. The longer poems contain shorter, folksong/ballad-like poems, to which I'll return.

One of Scott's earliest productions was *The Minstrelsy of the Scottish Border* of 1802/03, where his 'improvements' of Scottish ballads often make him as much author as editor of the collection.

(Several translations of the collection exist, not to mention innumerable translations of individual pieces scattered throughout early nineteenth-century European periodicals.) But prior to even *The Minstrelsy* Scott had made his own adaptations of German ballads. He even produced an English version of a Bosnian ballad, 'Hasanaginica' (Asan Aga's Wife), which he made over from Goethe's German translation. It's a grim tale of a woman who faces separation from her children because of the patriarchal tyranny of her husband and her brother. So, out of Europe Scott comes, and to Europe he returns, by way of balladry, and it's a ballad-hungry continent which discovers his work pre-*Waverley* and even post-*Waverley* if we take into account the many poems inserted in the novels. A large number of the translations of Scott are of the shorter ballad/folksong-like poems.

The Lady of the Lake, published in 1810, is Scott's debut as far his entirely original poetry is concerned. His biographer and son-in-law, J G Lockhart, quotes a comment to the effect that the poem virtually created the Scottish tourist industry: 'The whole country rang with the praises of the poet – crowds set off to view the scenery of Loch Katrine, till then comparatively unknown; and as the book came out just before the season for excursions, every house and inn in that neighbourhood was crammed with a constant succession of visitors.'

The poem's cult status spread to mainland Europe, and in a manner which belongs as much to the history of music as of literature. We can't easily divide history of music from history of literature, nor in my view should we. In an essay on the first Italian translations of Scott, Mary E Ambrose suggests that the 1813 *French* translation of *The Lady of the Lake* may have been the one which was drawn to the attention of the composer Rossini. In turn Rossini wrote the very first opera based on a Scott work, *La Donna del lago*, which was first performed in Naples in 1819. Scott's legacy in opera is a vast subject in itself and has been well documented in Jerome Mitchell's two volumes on the subject. Of course opera libretti take us much further down the line from translation to adaptation, but I would contend that if we're talking about reception of authors in other cultures, we do need to take into account the other arts – including musical settings – and visual imagery (engravings, paintings etc.) broadly illustrative of the texts.

There exist recordings of wonderful performances of Ellen's

(or Elena's) aria 'Tanti affetti' from Rossini's *La Donna del lago*. The King has become reconciled with Elena's father and has given up his romantic claim on her so that she can marry her long-term lover Malcolm. This aria concludes the opera and diverges totally from the text of the poem. Elena is overcome with so many joyful emotions; 'Tanti affetti in tal momento/ mi sa fanno al core intorno': she admits that she's so happy that she can't articulate her feelings. Nevertheless, this being opera, she has a damn good try.

Rossini's biographer, Stendhal, remarked on the visually powerful nature of the opening scene of the opera, with its décor suggesting the Highland loch, and Ellen gliding gracefully at the helm of her small boat.

Franz Schubert's biographer, Elizabeth Norman McKay, traces the next link in the chain of influence. She regards it as 'possible, if not probable' that Schubert had seen Rossini's opera sometime during 1823 or 1824. This would have been the spur for him to seek out the poem itself. He went on to make song-settings of Storck's translations of some of the lyrics within *The Lady of the Lake*, notably the three which carry the title 'Ellens Gesänge' and which culminate in the famous 'Ave Maria', based on Ellen's prayer towards the end of Canto Third. Elizabeth McKay writes that Schubert 'was awakened to a whole new world of romantic drama and emotion, in which tenderness and sensitivity coexisted with a larger, grander world of wide landscapes, nobility of mind, fateful action, and often tragic outcomes.'

Poland was one of the countries most enthusiastic about Scott, unsurprisingly given its strong cultural and political nationalism. Its leading national poet of the nineteenth century, Adam Mickiewicz, was to compose a long historical narrative, in verse, *Pan Tadeusz*, following the example of Scott. (Thirteen years ago I visited a Polish château whose garden is planted according to the plan laid out in *Pan Tadeusz*.) But the most notable Polish translation of *The Lady of the Lake* was made (under an assumed name) by Karol Sienkiewicz, the librarian to the Czartoryskis, a family who played a leading role in Polish culture and politics.

Literature can inspire sculpture. Loch Katrine, the setting of the poem, has been the source of Glasgow's water supply, and an elaborate Victorian fountain in the city's Kelvingrove Park, near the University, is a public-sculptural celebration of the poem, dating from 1872. The fountain is regarded – by the leading authority on

Glasgow's public sculptures – as being symbolic of Ellen's Isle in the middle of the loch.

On occasion Scott's poems were translated into prose. Conversely, in 1837, a major Czech writer turned certain chapters from a novel, *The Talisman*, into verse! The Scottish judge and historian, Lord Woodhouselee, took a very dim view of prose translations of poetry. In his *Essay on the Principles of Translation*, published in 1797, he wrote: 'To attempt [...] a translation of a lyric poem into prose, is the most absurd of all undertakings; for those very characters of the original which are essential to it, and which constitute its highest beauties, if transferred to a prose translation, become unpardonable blemishes. The excursive range of the sentiments, and the play of fancy, which we admire in the original, degenerate in the translation into mere raving and impertinence.'

In 1816 an editorial in the anglophile Swiss journal, the *Biblothèque universelle*, declared that it was difficult to find a French translation of Scott. It explained that the customs, history, local colour and other Scottish national characteristics were impossible to convey to the francophone reader. To understand Scott one had to learn English and also study the history of Scotland. Nevertheless, that didn't stop the same periodical from publishing, in the same year, the first of a substantial number of Scott extracts in French translation. And whatever the strictures of Lord Woodhouselee some twenty years earlier, the *Bibliothèque universelle* carried prose versions of the poems. One of these is of the ballad 'Rosabelle' which Scott inserted in *The Lay of the Last Minstrel*. It appears in Canto 6 of the poem. The heroine, Rosabelle, risks crossing the stormy Firth of Forth from the Fife side to join her lover in Lothian. Of course, her boat goes down and she becomes a prime example of Edgar Allan Poe's notion of the ultimate in tragedy, ie, the death of a young and beautiful woman.

Possibly the most interesting nineteenth-century translation of 'Rosabelle' is by Karolina Pavlova, Russia's major woman writer of the period. Pavlova was an accomplished woman who translated from several European languages (and translated Russian poetry *into* other languages), but in her native land she encountered hostility toward her work and also her personal life. Pavlova also translated the Scottish ballad 'Edward' as well as the ballad-like 'Glenara' by Thomas Campbell and many other short poems by Scott himself. This taste for ballads no doubt attracted her to

'Rosabelle' specifically, rather than to the longer poem of which it was a self-contained part.

Lay of the *Last* Minstrel: there's much in Scott's poetry that appeals to the pan-European vogue for sentimental melancholy. The notion of a bard who is the last of his race must have struck a chord with those whose attraction to the Macpherson/Ossian cult was still unabated by the early decades of the nineteenth century. (During my research days in the Biblioteca Naciónal, Madrid, I found a particularly awful Spanish verse encomium to Scott, crammed full of whining Ossianic bombast, in an early nineteenth-century periodical.)

Somewhat following on the line of *The Lay of the Last Minstrel*, *Rokeby*, another much-translated poem, contains passages of Gothic gloom, of Ossianic nostalgia for the former splendour of crumbling castles. *Rokeby* reached Russia, a country where translations of Macpherson and Scott are legion in the early nineteenth century. Mikhail Glinka, widely regarded as the father of Russian opera, was to go on to compose *Ruslan and Ludmila* and *A Life for the Tsar*, but his first contemplated operatic project was to be based on *Rokeby*. Only fragments remain. Before 1824 he wrote a song based on 'The Harp', one of the pieces in Canto 5 of Scott's poem – but he lost the MS. and rewrote it thirty years later from memory.

Забавы юношеских лет, весёлы хороводы,
Отчизны милый край моей и светлой Темзы воды,
Покинуть вас внушил кто мне несчастое желанье?
Я всем пожертвовал тебе, сердец очарованье,
Моя арфа!

It's interesting that the original poem takes up seven stanzas – here we have it conflated into one. Composers will take liberties generally with the text of a poem – necessarily, according to the demands of a musical aesthetic – so it's hardly surprising that, in a composer's hands, a *translated* poem will undergo even further metamorphosis away from the original.

Rokeby is a transitional poem in literary history in the sense that it's informed by pre-Romantic trappings, Ossianic and otherwise, but it looks forward to Byron – Bertram, the ex-pirate, is a precursor of the protagonists of *The Corsair* and *Lara*. (Byron was shortly to surpass Scott as a master of narrative verse).

Such transitional status is John Lauder's view in his book on Scott in the Twayne's English Authors Series; he also claims the eponymous protagonist of *Marmion* to be a pre-Byronic figure, although Scott in his opinion makes the mistake of spelling out Marmion's crime: no nobly and romantically mysterious outlaw he.

Very often the Scott poems chosen for translation do not register emphatically on the Scottish or British critical Richter scale. But I was pleased to see that one of Scott's most succinct verse narratives, *MacDuff's Cross*, had been accommodated in French and German guise, albeit in relatively obscure publications. It's one of his verse dramas and its relatively taut writing compares rather favourably with much in better-known works by Scott. I would speculate that it appealed to its European readers because of its evocation of a breathtakingly beautiful landscape (the view, from above Newburgh in Fife, across to Perthshire and the River Earn as it joins the Tay) together with its basis in folk legend.

Another example of unexpected but understandable reception would be the early Spanish and Portuguese translations of *The Vision of Don Roderick*, in which Scott pays tribute to the resilience of Spain and Portugal in the wake of Napoleonic depredations in the Iberian peninsula.

Within the past year I've done a lot of research, in Scotland and in central Europe, on the translations of traditional Scottish ballads. I mentioned earlier Karolina Pavlova's version of 'Edward, Edward'. Across Europe, especially in the smaller countries under imperial domination, there was much cultural-nationalist assertiveness of indigenous language and culture. Part of this involved the revival of folk ballads.

If, say, Bohemia and Poland wished to reinforce their own considerable ballad hoards, they could go to Scottish ballads – many of them to be found in Percy's *Reliques* or in Scott's *Minstrelsy* – and give them a make-over in their own languages, thereby adding to their existing ballad hoards, courtesy of Scotland.

A particularly ingenious appropriation was made by the Polish Romantic poet Juliusz Słowacki, in the course of his play on Mary Stuart, i.e. Mary Queen of Scots. In Act 5 the Queen is feeling guilty about having had her husband assassinated (Lord Darnley was her political rival as well as husband). To cheer her up, her page sings the ballad 'Edward'. Bad idea: for that ballad concerns a son who accuses his mother of having despatched his father. So, instead of feeling consoled, Mary feels only the more guilt. The Scottish ballads are concise, hard-edged, dramatically intense – ideal quarry for those occupied with creating a national literature.

In Bohemia, struggling for its identity under the Hapsburgs, the number of translations of the Scottish ballads has greatly exceeded what I'd expected at the outset. Towards the end of the nineteenth century, the Parnassian love of the finely-chiselled, together with the Symbolist love of the hauntingly atmospheric, may be contributory factors in Jaroslav Vrchlický's choice of Scottish material for his *Moderní básníci angličtí* [Modern English poetry] (Prague, 1898).

Vrchlický included a generous portion of *The Lady of the Lake* in Czech, together with his versions of a wide selection of Scott's shorter, ballad-like poems.

This broadly late-romantic response is discernible elsewhere. Across the Baltic, in Sweden, writers of the 1890s were reacting against the positivism and naturalism of the 1880s. There was in Sweden in the '90s a mood of *fin-de-siècle* Symbolism and an anti-rationalist regard for folklore and the presumed greater heroics of pre-nineteenth-century Swedish and world history. A leading figure here is Gustaf Fröding, a *poète maudit* with troubles related to both his loins and his liver. He translated Burns (himself notoriously loins-and-liver-vulnerable), and although he did not actually *translate* Scott he found in him an expansive antidote to the mundane, humdrum materialism of late nineteenth-century Sweden, and this animated his own poetry, which explicitly offers theme and variation on motifs from Scott's works.

Peter Graves, a Scandinavian Studies colleague at Edinburgh, has specialised in Fröding's *original* poetry on Scott-inspired themes. As for counterparts of such a phenomenon in other languages, that's a promising area for further research.

Castle Corbie

'I have trod the upward and the downward slope': for me, it was an unabashed nostalgia trip, as precipitous Meylan had been one of my temporary homes. It's due north of the university campus at Grenoble, where I first taught back in 1993. That was the spring semester of that year, and I'm currently here for the autumn of 2011, so I've been curious to revisit Meylan and see a fadingly familiar haunt in (to me) its unfamilar garb of this season.

I'd forgotten it was so steep: obviously I was a lot younger nineteen years ago – cue a T S Eliot parody (do you know it?): 'As we get oldah we do not get any youngah' – but I like to think I'm just as fit. *Qu'importe*: I was determined to make my way to Berlioz's Scottish castle. For just before my first posting here, composer Ronald Stevenson had told me that Berlioz came from the part of France to which I was headed.

I didn't realise, then, just how near my digs would be to key sites associated with the composer of the *Rob Roy* and *Waverley* overtures. This quiet suburb of Grenoble is packed with historical meaning. A memorial marks the spot where a group of Resistance fighters was executed by the Nazi occupiers. Stendhal, who maintained a love-hate relationship with his native Grenoble, wrote praise-prose-poetry to the sheer rock faces east of the city and the expansive glen of the Grésivaudan over which Meylan is perched. The final scene of Berlioz's *La damnation de Faust* has our eponymous hero singing of the rough terrain that echoes his mood as he awaits Mephistopheles for the last time. In that music you can hear the landscape that Berlioz knew from his youth.

Just up the road from my old quarters is the former house of Berlioz's maternal grandfather, Nicolas Marmion. Yes – you read that right: Walter Scott is the not-very-sub subtext of all this. Berlioz, like other young French Romantics of his time, was avidly reading the Wizard of the North, and a ruined tower to the north of Marmion's house gave him, in imagination, something of the Scotland which he would never visit in that dull dimension which we call real life.

It was in grandfather Marmion's house, at a party, that the 12-year-old Berlioz fell in love with an 18-year-old guest, Estelle, who wanted to dance with the little fellow, and later take him on

Sunday walks up the slope. Out of this bittersweet experience came the *idée fixe* of the *Symphonie fantastique*. In his sixties, the composer traced her to Geneva: both, by then, were widowed, but Estelle gently told him that it was now too late. You can read all about it in his memoirs, but be aware that these often stray from that dull dimension cited above.

As does, no doubt, his Scottish tower. Yesterday it was misty, so visibility on these wooded crags was much less than it had been when I was here with visiting wife and daughter in the spring of '93. I had a detailed map, but as I climbed nearer, I was puzzled. A woman coming from her house saw me peering at the map and wanted to help. Was I looking for Château Corbeau? She directed me to a pebbly track heading up into the forest.

Château Corbeau – let's appropriate it as Castle Corbie - is a gloomy place, a tumbled wall entwined with roots and branches. I clambered over it, thinking that it wasn't so much a *Rob Roy* or *Waverley* setting - it was more redolent of the ballads collected by Scott in his *Minstrelsy of the Scottish Border*, or of his own shorter verse narratives. In the thickening mist, the cafés of Grenoble seemed a world away. More distant yet, in so many senses, was our actually-existing Scotland.

Byron in Love

Edna O'Brien introduces Byron by way of his comments on Burns, which (like others before her) she sees as a self-portrait: 'tenderness, roughness delicacy, coarseness – sentiment, sensuality… dirt and deity – all mixed up in that one compound of inspired clay.'

Step forward, First Lord of the Caledonian Antisyzygy. Byron's initially arresting phrase on himself-via-Burns was 'an antithetical mind'. His boyhood in Aberdeen would seem to bear it all out: the angry wee street-loun, with his Doric 'Dinna speak o' it!', who had become the posh Harrow-educated aristo, imbibing from his nurse, pretty well simultaneously, Calvinism and sex. Not that we should equate Calvinism with puritanism. One suspects that Geordie Byron would be a less outrageous figure in 1790s Protestant Aberdeen than in the 1950s Catholic Ireland against which Edna O'Brien has so eloquently rebelled. There's a dark sensuality in Calvinist culture, throbbing as it does through the speeches of the doomed protagonist of *Manfred* (1817). O'Brien quotes Goethe's praise for its 'heavenly hue of words': Goethe valued Byron as a poet (not at all as a thinker), and in *Faust* Part Two based the tragic Euphorion, son of Faust and Helen of Troy, on the ex-Aberdoninn.

Yes, this was the man whose nobility was a matter of character as much as of class, who could stand up in the House of Lords and speak passionately for the starving workers: 'Will you erect a gibbet in every field, and hang up men like scarecrows?' This was also the man who treated his hapless daughter Allegra 'with contemptuous cruelty'. Here, Edna O'Brien may have reflected ruefully on her failed relationship with her own father.

The title of this biography reflects the preoccupations of its author's fiction. To borrow Muriel Spark's phrase for Rose Stanley in *The Prime of Miss Jean Brodie*, Edna O'Brien is 'famous for sex'. (As indeed was James Joyce, subject of an earlier biography by this author.) In many ways, O'Brien's Byron complements that of Allan Massie, in the latter's *Byron's Travels* (1988), which appeared in the year of the poet's bicentenary. Inevitably and quite properly the two biographies overlap. often quoting from the same sources. However, as befits a noted commentator on politics and history, Massie makes more of the public dimension of Byron's life and art. In a 2003 interview O'Brien maintained that 'everything is political... whether we like it or not': essentially, though, the 'political' for her is focused on sexuality and its vexed relationship with religion. That constitutes much of the matter of Ireland: in no other west European country, perhaps, is there such an antagonism of feminism towards nationalism – understandably, in view of the latter's close association with patriarchal Catholicism.

O'Brien records that, in Milan, Byron 'met the shy young Stendhal'. Massie makes rather more of the encounter between the two great anti-romantie romantics of the post-Waterloo years. For both men, the fallen Napoleon had acquired enormous mythic significance. In Stendhal's *Le Rouge et le Noir* (1830), the handsome chancer Julien Sorel contemplates a Napoleon-like eagle above the Jura, and is himself seen as a charismatic force of nature. Bored with the mincing mediocrities of the Restoration salons, the impressionable Mlle de la Mole remarks to herself anent Julien: 'Dans ce siècle, ou toute énergie est morte, son énergie leur fait peur.' This should explain why Stendhal was so swoony in the presence of Byron. With Napoleon no longer around, Byron seemed the inheritor of the Corsican's 'énergie', the hope for deliverance from the conformist, reactionary hegemonies of the 1810s and 1820s.

But just before everyone gets a bit too carried away by these heady associations, they are comically undercut in a way that Stendhal (in his wryer and more customary moments) might have appreciated. [Byron] reckoned,' notes O'Brien, 'that already he had given more to the Greek cause than that with which Bonaparte had begun his Italian campaign'. In 1980 the critic George O'Brien (no relaton) remarked on the 'sense of tearful farcicality' in Edna O'Brien's fiction: it is precisely that which so animates her biography of Byron – the juxtaposition of rhapsodic sentiment with ruthless shagging; the grieving Greeks who, 'wishing for the heart to be left there, were given instead his lungs und larynx, which were placed in an urn and stolen not long afterwards'. Byron could be the poseur who, according to Rowan Atkinson's Blackadder, swanned around Italy in order to get laid; he could also be the acute bullshit-detector, possessing an eighteenth-century wit closer in spirit to Pope than to his contemporaries such as Shelley (though the latter's *Swellfoot the Tyrant* not only comes close to Byron's satirical mode but arguably surpasses it).

In his memorable Aberdeen lectures, which had something of a dry Calvinistic air about them, the late Andrew Rutherford was typically lucid in his preference for Byron the anti-romantic over Byron the romantic. O'Brien's Byron is not quite so clear-cut, not so either/or, but is viewed through an Irish sensibility that picks up on both the melancholy and the madness. As we would expect, she has much to say on your man's long-suffering Irish friend, the subject of Byron's gossip, 'the small ribbings that he could never resist, saying that Tom Moore's verses were so very sweet because his father, a Dublin grocer, had fed him sugar plums as a child'.

Pushkin in Scotland

In 1917, the year in which the study of Russian was inaugurated at Glasgow University, its Principal made a statement that would prove to be prophetic. Sir Donald MacAlister, a man of wide abilities and interests – a true polymath – expressed his desire that translators in Scotland might address themselves to Russian poetry, and requested them to make such versions in English and Scots.

The University's Slavonic section has gone on to answer that call in its publications and public events, and beyond the Glasgow campus a landmark event was the appearance, in 2014, of *After Lermontov* (Carcanet Press), an anthology of translations – in English and Scots – of poetry by Mikhaïl Lermontov (1814-41), who was descended from the Scottish Learmonth family. The Scotland-Russia Forum is actively promoting Russian culture in our country, and the Russian-themed events at Moffat in the Scottish Borders have also operated both within and beyond academia.

Lermontov and Alexander Pushkin (1799-1837) are considered to be the two most outstanding Russian poets of the early nineteenth century. It's instructive to focus on how two Scottish poets – Edwin Morgan (1920-2010) and Alastair Mackie (1925-95) – have addressed themselves to an unfinished but atmospheric Pushkin poem which in English has the title 'Autumn'. Its first stanza – indeed the whole existing poem – looks forward to the serene evocations of landscape and nature in the fiction of Ivan Turgenev (best known for the novel *Fathers and Children*) and the paintings of Isaac Levitan who was a friend of Anton Chekhov.

For Pushkin, the autumn is to be preferred to the spring, but the generally celebratory tone of the poem takes a tragic turn with the comparison of autumn to a consumptive young girl, as here in Edwin Morgan's version:

She smiles still, with red lips that fade to grey;
Her face has twilight in its blood, not dawn […]

The last and twelfth stanza of this fragmentary poem consists of only one line but Edwin Morgan adds to it five lines of his own:

Great to sail off with it [a ship]. But where to go?
What lands shall we now see: vast Caucasus,
Or some sun-blistered Moldavian meadow,
Or Normandy's snow-gleaming policies,
Or Switzers' pyramid array on show,
Or wild and sad Scottish rock-fortresses... ?

That splendid if somewhat gratuitous reference to Scottish castles seems closer to Lermontov than to Pushkin! Lermontov's awareness of his Scottish ancestry led him to compose a poem 'A Wish' in which he evoked a fantasy Scottish castle. Lermontov had never visited Scotland, but he had read his Walter Scott, as indeed had Pushkin.

So Edwin Morgan is here deploying the Pushkin poem – and why not? – as a springboard for what seems almost to be the beginning of another poem – an original Morgan poem. However, it's Alastair Mackie who engages even further in this manner with the Pushkin poem.

Mackie doesn't actually give us a translation of the whole poem. He quotes individual lines; and yes, he gives us his Scots version of the first stanza of Pushkin's poem – but that constitutes the second stanza of his original poem 'At the Back-End' ['back-end' = autumn]. Here, then, we have eight lines of Pushkin via Mackie, followed by two lines of Mackie speaking for himself:

'October's set in syne; the hinmaist leaves
o the shaw shak fae their strippit branches.
There's a cauld nip in the souch o Aatumn.
The road's freezin; and jist beyond the mill
the burn rins blabberin but the pond's gealed ower.
My neebor's up and aff to the huntin fields
bladdin the winter craps wi his deavin pack
o dugs yowlin, waukenin the wids' deep sleep.'
Pushkin's back-end poems. I browse amang his drauchts
and pen my ain texts for the lang mirk nichts.

Note that 'pen my *ain* [own] texts', and before that 'his drauchts' [drafts, sketches], Mackie's recognition that Pushkin's 'Autumn' is an incomplete work.

It's as if a fragmentary poem calls on other poets to complete it, as in Edwin Morgan's case, or to use it as a theme on which to compose a set of variations, as a composer would treat a piece of somebody else's music. This is what Mackie is doing with the Pushkin poem. His 'variations' have the effect of transposing Pushkin's four seasons to Scotland, and he dwells especially on how cold the country can be during autumn and winter.

Alastair Mackie alludes to Robert Henryson's *The Testament of Cresseid*, which begins with that late medieval Scottish poet warming himself by the fire during the virulent Fife winter. There are also references in 'At the Back-End', *passim*, to a range of European cultural figures including Baudelaire and Homer, but Mackie keeps coming back to the Scottish canon, including the ballads, and to Pushkin himself.

A major theme in Pushkin's poetry is the transitoriness of human life; for example, there is the image in one poem of an ancient oak-tree, which was there before the poet was born and which will still be there after his death – and after his times. That's a theme which is very strong in Scottish poetry, and Alastair Mackie quotes another late medieval Scots makar, William Dunbar: 'On to the deid gois all estatis'.

Mackie was the son of an Aberdeen quarryman, and many of his poems turn on the experience of growing up in the city during the 1930s. He evokes working-class life in Aberdeen with his characteristic blend of humour and melancholy, and in a rich Doric to which he adds a wider Scots vocabulary. His adult life was spent mainly in Anstruther in the East Neuk of Fife, where he taught English at Waid Academy. It was here that he nurtured pupils such Christopher Rush who would go on to make their literary mark and to pay fond tribute to their mentor.

The East Neuk has links to the ancestors of Mikhaïl Lermontov, for example at Balcomie Castle by Crail, near the easternmost edge of Fife. The county, as it were, points in the direction of Russia. However, as Mackie lived by the sea, the imagery of his poetry is essentially coastal, in contrast to Pushkin whose loci are far inland, except for a maritime image in stanza 11 of the Russian's poem 'Autumn'.

Moreover, a major departure from Pushkin is Mackie's preference for summer: the Scottish poet cites Pushkin's dislike of that season, with its dust, its flies and dry fields. (Readers of Dostoyevsky's *Crime and Punishment* may be reminded of the stifling St Petersburg summers endured by the intellectual murderer Raskolnikov.) As for Mackie, though, as it's so cold in Scotland for much of the year, he is only too glad when the sun comes out.

As 'At the Back-End' nears its conclusion, Mackie takes up Pushkin's image of the pale young woman dying of consumption as somehow appropriate to autumn. The Scot sees his own country's autumn very differently, as a season of intense light contrasting with the mist (the *haar*, as we call it in Fife), as a season of 'caller amplitudes / o sea and sky'. To Mackie, autumn is a season which is very conducive to the writing of poetry. In his last stanza Mackie echoes Pushkin's line 'Pen beckons to finger, paper to pen' (as Edwin Morgan translates it). Sitting by the fire in his study, Mackie puts it thus: 'My biro yokey [itchy, impatient] atween the forefinger / and thoom [thumb].'

Alastair Mackie concludes 'At the Back-End' with a 'makar's handshak' – a poet's handshake - with his fellow-poet Pushkin: here is the solidarity of fellow-artists. Pushkin's 'Autumn', together with Morgan's translation and Mackie's variations on themes, concerns the effects of nature, and of the seasons, on human creativity – as well as, conversely, how that creativity transmutes nature into art.

Ivan Turgenev in Scotland

At the banquet in the Corn Exchange on Edinburgh's Grassmarket, the guest speaker rose to his feet. 'Of all that sacred legion of great men,' he declared, 'who, though foreign to its soil, have taken part in the intellectual development of Russia, no-one perhaps has earned more gratitude, has gained more affection, than Walter Scott, and proud and happy am I to be this day the interpreter to Scott's compatriots of that affection and that gratitude'.

The audience cheered, but the speaker felt that all was not well. He had been uncertain and nervous in his delivery. English, after all, was not his native tongue (and the above text is based on a newspaper report which he later corrected). Was that crowd before him really all that interested in Russian literature? When the toastmaster had announced him as 'Mr Turkeynuff', it felt ominous.

For Ivan Sergeyevich Turgenev (1818-1883), the distinguished Russian novelist, the Scott Centenary of 1871 ought to have been an occasion of unalloyed delight. He was staying at the Caledonian Hotel and from his room could have enjoyed the view of his literary hero's city. The train journey from King's Cross, however, had worn him out, the heat was oppressive, he felt lonely and anxious as he made his way to the Grassmarket.

If only he could have found comfort in the thought that his English was likely to be better than his audience's Russian.

His masterpiece *Fathers and Children* (1862) is one of the key works of Russian literature. As the title suggests, it concerns tensions between the young and the old, and how those relate to the conflicts in society as a whole: the private sphere is a microcosm of the public sphere. In this novel, the older generation guards its romantic idealism, its taste for the arts; the younger, represented by the brisk and intense Bazarov, holds equally fast to a hard-headed practicality and to scientific solutions to social ills – 'A decent chemist,' he insists 'is twenty times more useful than any poet'. The fathers are too sentimental and nostalgic; the children look to a drastically transformative future.

Walter Scott's historical novels had set the standard for fictional characters who were at once convincingly individualised and at the same time representative of their class in times of great upheaval.

Their personal trajectories, however unique in details, were still true to type. In *Rob Roy* (1817), the eponymous hero – or should that be ex-hero – is of the waning clan system and is memorably confronted by his kinsman Bailie Nicol Jarvie, the quintessential member of the rising urban bourgeoisie.

The parallels with *Fathers and Children* are clear, but Turgenev may not necessarily have been conscious of them: Patrick Waddington in his misguidingly titled *Turgenev in England* (1981), to which I'm indebted for his account of our man's Scottish *séjour*, argues that Turgenev's understanding of Scott was too romantic, naïve, insufficiently ironic. (It was, one might add, a quite un-Bazarovian response).

Following the Edinburgh débâcle, Turgenev headed up to Pitlochry. 'Nowhere in the world is there such an air,' he wrote, 'as in the north of Scotland; it is a joy to breathe it'. He proceeded to Loch Tummel and to the glorious Twelfth: one wonders if in his gun sights, as he blasted away, he would have had a vision of his Edinburgh audience. Even the shoot, however, was a disappointment to someone from a country where it was part of the rural culture.

His book of short stories, *Sketches from a Hunter's Album* (1852), with its compassionate treatment of the country folk (if not of its wildlife) is believed to have contributed to the mood which led to the abolition of serfdom in 1861. The lyricism of the stories, and their evocation of the Russian landscape, look forward to the short fiction of Anton Chekhov and to the paintings of Chekhov's friend Isaac Levitan.

As for that later writer's reception in Scotland, it has proved to be more successful than Turgenev's experience of his own welcome. Nevertheless Alan Bennett reports, in his *Untold Stories* (2005), an actor friend's witness when playing Chekhov in Edinburgh, and afterwards overhearing a lady member of the audience, who remarked: 'There was a lot of laughter at the end of the first act, but I soon put a stop to that'. Moreover, the same actor was appearing at Perth in Chekhov's best-known play, and noted an unawareness of its inexorably doomed trees: the production was billed as *The Cheery Orchard*. Perhaps the Russians could be conceded the last laugh at such insularity.

Carlyle, France and Germany in 1870

Perhaps the best-known literary response to the Franco-Prussian War is Emile Zola's *La Débâcle* (1892). The main female character, Henriette Weiss, has left her home in the provinces in order to seek her brother in the capital. At a railway station north of the city, she encounters a Prussian officer; from their vantage point on a footbridge over the tracks, they view a Paris in flames. Henriette demands of the Prussian: what have we done to be punished in this way?

> Otto raised his arm in a peremptory gesture. He was about to speak, with all the vehemence of his harsh, military, Bible-quoting puritanism. But, glancing at the young woman beside him, the calm intelligence of her gaze made him change his mind, though his gesture in itself had been enough to betray his feeling of racial hatred, his conviction that he was here in France as a judge, sent by the god of war to chastise a depraved people. Paris was being burnt down as a punishment for centuries of loose living, for the crimes and debauchery committed over the years, and once again Germany would save the world by purging it of the last traces of Latin corruption.

The Prussian officer could almost be echoing the sentiments of Thomas Carlyle at the fall of France after its crushing defeat at Sedan on 1st September 1870. Carlyle's values of duty and earnestness, bred into him in Calvinistic Scotland, perfectly accorded with Lutheran Prussia. He prized discipline above the frivolous, loose-living ways of Latin France. Surely France had been overdue for another 'true Apocalypse', a phoenix-like necessary death by fire, such as he had chronicled in *The French Revolution* over thirty years earlier.

Accordingly, and against a developing feeling in Britain that France had been brutally treated by a more powerful neighbour, Carlyle fired off a letter to *The Times*. In this polemic, published on 18th November 1870, he accused France of having been the aggressor —indeed, of having been for centuries the initiator of conflicts with Germany. The letter was influential and was much translated.

Carlyle maintained that Bismarck, the Prussian minister-president and imperial chancellor-in-waiting, was perfectly entitled to reclaim the provinces of Alsace and Lorraine (which, over the next seventy-five years, would be to-ing and fro-ing between French and German rule). The French were 'sanguinary mountebanks'. Bismarck, however, was welding a nation which would become Queen of the Continent, instead of vapouring, vainglorious, gesticulating. quarrelsome, restless and over-sensitive France. Here was the worthy successor of Frederick the Great, subject of Carlyle's recent historical opus: in Bismarck, Carlyle had apparently found a new Hero for 1870, as against France the arch-Dandy.

Carlyle's letter represents the full development of a leitmotiv that had been recurring throughout his work – his identification of a major fault-line in European culture between north and south, Teuton and Latin. The polar opposites in more recent European history have been east and west, as demonstrated by recent events in the Balkans.

Certainly during the nineteenth century, the likes of Dostoyevsky would posit a messianic Russian nationalism as a counterforce to western materialism; on the whole, however, the prevailing dialectic was north-south.

To a considerable extent this corresponds to Carlyle's scorn for (French) Enlightenment scepticism in favour of the Everlasting Yea of German idealism, such as we find in his markedly moralistic interpretation of the works of Goethe. Granted, Voltaire does not receive a completely bad press from Carlyle – the author of *Candide*, after all, was a mentor to Frederick the Great - but the Scotsman deplores the Frenchman's lack of earnestness and reverence. Voltaire, he writes, wields a torch for burning, not a hammer for building. To Carlyle, Voltaire is a mocker, a denier. In Goethe's *Faust*, Part 1, Mephistopheles introduces himself as the spirit who denies: Carlyle considered Mephistopheles to bear a curious resemblance to the archetypal French Enlightenment *philosophe*.

In Carlyle's view, the Enlightenment, by its reductivism, its scepticism, its Nay-Saying, had created the Mechanical Age. On the other hand German idealism, via Goethe, had offered hope in a new organicism. a revived Tree of Ygdrasil versus the clanking of the World-Machine. (Goethe was a student of the metamorphosis of plants.) The Mechanical Age had reduced men to mere parts of machines; against such fragmentation, Goethe represented the ideal of the whole man, both poet and man of action. Indeed, back in the 1820s, Carlyle had asserted that Goethe's poetry 'is no separate faculty, no mental handicraft; but the voice of the whole harmonious manhood'. Goethe possesses 'an eye and a heart equally for the sublime, the common and the ridiculous.' It was as if, for Carlyle, a France which lacked faith in an Everlasting Yea, in the sublime, could feast only on the common and the ridiculous. It was as if French art was anti-holistic, no more than the product of a 'separate faculty', a mere 'mental handicraft' – an essentially dilettante affair, self-indulgently sensual. French literature, he fumed, was 'infernal stuff'; it was 'a new kind of Phallus-worship' with such as Balzac for its prophets.

The meretricious régime of Napoleon III had been, for Carlyle, the nadir of a culture of effeminacy. As for the metropolitan centre of that culture, it was 'nothing but a brothel and a gambling Hell'; Parisians were 'a vain dancing-master sort of people'. During his visit to France in 1851, shortly before Louis-Napoleon's coup d'état that led ultimately to the abolition of the Second Republic and the creation of the Second Empire, Carlyle scoffed at the uniforms of those French soldiers whom he encountered on the Champ de Mars. He loathed the design of French military dress, such as the 'ridiculous flower-pot caps'. In 1870 the French would indeed preen themselves on their uniforms as they went to war, in contrast to the practical Prussians who were more concerned to deploy the new railway system as an integral part of modern warfare. There is the irony, which has not gone unnoticed, that Carlyle, the opponent of mechanism, could so admire the Prussian military machine. A second irony is that whereas Napoleon III admired his writings, Carlyle was in no mind to be gracious to his fan, dismissing the Emperor for his 'scandalous Copper-Captaincy'. (During his English exile, Louis-Napoleon, as he then was, had actually visited Carlyle in Chelsea.)

In 1870, Carlyle rejoiced at the triumph of the masculine, patriarchal *Heldenpolitik* of the future 'Iron' Chancellor who would shortly usher in a new, united German Empire. However, at an International Thomas Carlyle Symposium held in Germany in 1981, G Ross Roy cited evidence that, subsequently, Carlyle became more sympathetic to France; indeed, during the 1870s, he was guardedly impressed with the work of the French historian Jules Michelet, who had produced a magnum opus on the Revolution. Carlyle acknowledged France's virtues of grace and elegance, especially in its language, which 'so many [of its] neighbours learn: one great advantage over Poland, but not an all-availing one.'(Carlyle is a master at praising with faint damnation.)

He could on occasion damn as well as praise Germany, using such words as 'prosy' and 'dull'. After all, the Dryasdust historians whom he took to task in Frederick the Great were German historians. The award to him of the Prussian Order of Merit he found a pompous business – describing it, he uses the Scots word 'fash' in its sense of 'hassle' (somewhat ironically, it derives from the French *fâcher*). In a letter to his brother Alexander he writes that if the Prussians had sent him a quarter pound of good tobacco he'd have been a lot happier!

One has a sense that in Carlyle's Prussian triumphalism there is something that seems, in retrospect, rather Pyrrhic. Granted, a few years later Wagner would stage the ultra-German *Ring* cycle at Bayreuth, following up the musical revolution initiated by *Tristan und Isolde*. This would seem to be the cultural counterpart to Germany's political and military hegemony, to the new European order. However, that very cultural dominance would be curiously short-lived. It was France which would prove the world cultural leader by the end of the century, having by then ended its flirtation with Wagnerism in favour of its own home-grown avant-garde. It was a north German, Friedrich Nietzsche, who sought to restore the cultural appeal of the Latin world at the expense of the Nordic. He dispelled the thick mists of Wagner's *Ring* in order to bring forth the luminous Mediterranean world of Bizet's *Carmen*.

Nietzsche had no time for Carlyle – the rapturous *Übermensch* or Overman (anti-)philosophy of the former was far from the earnest, dyspeptic *Helden*-worship of the latter. Having come to despise all things Teutonic, Nietzsche would hardly be favourable towards a Scotsman who in so many ways tried to be more German than the Germans.

Debut at Antwerp: The Flanders Chapters of Robert Louis Stevenson's *An Inland Voyage*

In the summer of 1896, two young Scotsmen set off for a journey by canoe along the waterways of Belgium and northern France. One was Robert Louis Stevenson (RLS), a writer who had contributed to periodicals but had yet to publish his first book, of which the trip itself was to furnish the subject matter.

His companion was Walter Simpson, son of Sir James, the discoverer of chloroform. These would-be adventurers belonged to respectable middle-class Edinburgh families; for a while, at least, they wanted to forget the fact. From upper windows in the staid burghers' homes of the New Town, younger and livelier residents could be tantalised by a panorama of the Forth estuary and the North Sea: clearly there were escape routes.

Not that 'home' and 'abroad' were altogether distinct from each other. Travel, to Stevenson, presented a strange paradoxical mix of the familiar and the unfamiliar. For example, in his latter years in the South Pacific, he'd exchange folk tales with his native hosts and marvel at the 'kinship' between Scottish and Polynesian traditions and peoples. His boyhood visits to the coast of Fife would expose him to Flemish-Dutch-style architecture, crow-step gables and all, long before he disembarked at Flanders itself.

I am writing this article in my Fife home not far from Dysart, which for Stevenson brought back memories of 'the Dutch ships that lay in its harbour, painted like toys and with pots of flowers and cages of song birds in the cabin windows, and for one particular Dutch skipper who would sit all day in slippers on the break of the poop, smoking a long German pipe'. The closing chapters of *Catriona* (1893), the sequel to *Kidnapped*, are not lacking in romantic drama as the lovers make their way from Helvoetsluys to Dunkirk, but we also carry away impressions of Low Countries domesticity, as snug as any Edinburgh chimney-corner: 'Indeed, there was much for Scots folk to admire: canals and trees being intermingled with the houses; the houses, each within itself, of a brave red brick, the colour of a rose, with steps and benches of blue marble at the cheek of every door, and the whole town so clean you might have dined upon the causeway. Sprott was within, upon his ledgers, in a low parlour, very neat and clean, and set out with China and pictures and a globe of the earth in a brass frame'. Stevenson's sail on the Willebroek Canal must have reminded him of Scotland: for most of the time, it rained.

An Inland Voyage appeared in 1878, with a frontispiece by the artist and illustrator Walter Crane. From the very first paragraph of this, Stevenson's first book, there's a sense of liberation:

> We made a great stir in Antwerp Docks. A stevedore and a lot of dock porters took up the two canoes, and ran with them for the slip. A crowd of children followed cheering. The *Cigarette* went off in a splash and a bubble of small breaking water. Next moment the *Arethusa* was after her. A steamer was coming down, men on the paddle-box shouted hoarse warnings, the stevedore and his porters were bawling from the quay. But in a stroke or two the canoes were away out in the middle of the Scheldt, and all steamers, and stevedores, and other 'long-shore' vanities were left behind.

They find themselves in a landscape both rural and industrial: 'Here and there was a pleasant village among trees, with a noisy shipping yard; here and there a villa in a lawn'. Turning from the Scheldt into the Rupel, they glide leisurely past a riverbank still green and pastoral, with alleys of trees along the embankment, and here and there a flight of steps to serve a 'ferry', before they reach the drab brickyards of Boom. Stevenson is more than a little cheeky on the dour denizens of the local botel. The fare proves to be no introduction to Belgian *haute casine*, of which Stevenson will remain unconvinced: 'they seem to peck and trifle with viands all day long in an amateur spirit tentatively French, truly German, and somehow falling between the two'. Yet the voyagers' own cooking, *al fresco* over an Etna stove, is less than brilliant: an accidentally smashed egg is prepared in its covering of Flemish newspaper, to emerge as 'a cold and sordid *fricassé* of printer's ink and broken egg-shell'. However, in true Scottish style, they can blame their failure on the weather.

RLS is fascinated by barges, and speculates on the life of those on board, He remarks – enviously – that the bargee can simultaneously travel and stay at home. 'He may take his afternoon walk in some foreign country on the banks of the canal, and then come bome to dinner at his own fireside'. Stevenson is projecting his own deepest yearnings, caught as he is between conflicting impulses to rove and to bide; elsewhere he declares that 'to travel hopefully is a better thing than to arrive'. Even better, it seems, is to travel homefully.

It's arguable that RLS is romanticising. He's on vacation, not so the bargee. In the Musée des Beaux-Arts at Tournai/Doornik there's a painting by Theodoor Verstraete, *De bootrekker/Barge Hauler* (1890). The solitary figure on the towpath may be proceeding at the slow pace of which Stevenson approves, but that's because it requires exertion to pull the vessel along.

The bargee is a convenient symbol of RLS's bid for freedom from sedentary routine; he'd rather be a bargee 'than occupy any position under Heaven that required attendance at an office'. The bargee has been appointed an honorary bohemian. During the later French part of their voyage, the two Scots are invited aboard a barge whose 'good people' boast of 'their happy condition in life, as if they had been Emperor and Empress of the Indies'. Stevenson admires folk who don't whine about their poverty. Is this a dilettante Victorian condescension towards the contented lower orders? To an extent perhaps; yet we might give RLS the credit for his graceful tribute to the dignity and independence of those who ply Europe's canals.

An Inland Voyage articulates Stevenson's belief that if poverty is accompanied by freedom, it's more attractive than wealth constrained by respectability. He advocates a tatterdemalion existentialism. 'To know what you prefer, instead of humbly saying Amen to what the world tells you you ought to prefer, is to have kept your soul alive'. It's curious how the 1960s overlooked RLS as a potential guru.

We shouldn't philosophise heavily upon a philosophy that is anything but heavy. When *An Inland Voyage* was first published, it was commended for its relaxed tone: 'While your tourist is perspiring inquiringly about with his Murray [guidebook] and his binocular, poking his nose into altar-pieces and cricking his neck in efforts of architectural intelligence, this young man is smoking a pipe on the ramparts, or talking to the people in the inn-parlour'. So let's rejoin the two Scots as they head easy-osily towards Brussels, cropheaded children spitting on them from the bridges as they pass below.

Along the banks, they are ignored by fishermen who are no les immobile 'than if they had been fishing in an old Dutch print'. The rain starts again, falling 'in straight, parallel lines, and the surface of the coal was thrown into an infinity of little crystal fountains'. The chapter closes with this superb description:

Beautiful country houses with clocks and long lines of shuttered windows, and fine old trees standing in grooves and avenues, gave a rich and sombre aspect in the rain and the deepening dusk to the shores of the canal. I seem to have seen something of the same effect in engravings: opulent landscapes, deserted and overhung with the passage of storm. And throughout we had the escort of a hooded cart, which trotted shabbily along the tow-path, and kept at an almost uniform distance in our wake.

Reviewing the book, Sidney Colvin remarked: 'These descriptions are not in the nature of an inventory of facts; it is a landscape-writing like the landscape-painting of the Japanese, setting down this or that point that happens to have made itself vividly felt, and leaving the rest: so that another traveller might go the same journey and scarcely notice any of the same things.'

Some twenty years later, another young Scot was to interpret the same part of the world with equal limpidity: in 1899 the Dundonian artist George Dutch Davidson (1879–1901) produced his impressions in prose: 'We were sailing up the Scheldt. The country looks distinctly foreign and I found it very interesting no doubt because it is extremely decorative. There are no woods – the trees are placed in long straight lines at regular distances apart, and the foliage assumes some very nice forms... I could never have conceived houses so like toy ones – no, not even in a sampler design'. Davidson the verbal painter complements Stevenson the visual writer.

Stevenson begins *An Inland Voyage* at Antwerp with a short dramatic sentence, and likewise opens his last Belgian chapter: 'The rain took off near Laeken.' In Brussels Stevenson and Simpson have a comically matey encounter with the young enthusiasts of the Royal Sport Nautique. The Scots decide that they lack the stamina and seriousness of their Belgian counterparts; rather than negotiate the fifty-five locks between Brussels and Charleroi, they opt to reach the French border by train. When the plucky recognise their limitations, let us not call them wimps.

It would be a good many years before Stevenson's wanderings would test him to the utmost, before he 'should fulfil the Scots destiny throughout, and live a voluntary exile'. He wrote thus, to Sidney Colvin, from his final base in Samoa, the letter is dated August 1893, a little over a year before his death. His 1876 inland voyage could have nothing of the finality of his later island voyage. Inland and island differ by one letter 'n' is replaced by 's', north is replaced by south, one polar attraction eventually winning out over another. On the canals, though, Stevenson and his companion found themselves temporarily in one northern setting (Flanders) that was hardly remote from another (Scotland). The native would return, to discover 'what rearrangements fortune had perfected the while in our surroundings; what surprises stood ready made for us at home; and whither and how far the world had voyaged in our absence'.

Margaret Oliphant's *A Beleaguered City*

Margaret Oliphant (1828-97) was a seemingly contradictory figure: assertive of the independence of strong women like herself, but at the same time conservative in her general cultural, social and religious outlook.

She was steeped in French literature and culture, but there were severe limits to her admiration. Scottish Presbyterian rectitude kicked in. She was a devout member of the Church of Scotland and did not care for novels about illicit sex. She had a dry, sardonic way of dealing with her dislikes, and Thomas Hardy's *Two on a Tower* and *Jude the Obscure* were sitting targets for her. Her distaste for French 'yellow-backed' novels is pretty commonplace for her time – you didn't have to be an uptight Scot to loathe filthy French books; you could just as well be an uptight Englishman/woman.

She was withering on Zola and Maupassant. Her tone isn't one of po-faced indignation; she goes in rather for the stylish put-down. In her own fiction, she has certain characters who spend a lot of time reading French 'yellow-backs': these folk are portrayed as idle and self-indulgent. (Another writer from a Puritan culture, though possessive of a worldly cosmopolitanism – Henry James – took such criticism to a pitch of refined sting: '[T]here is something ineffably odd', he writes of the brothers Goncourt, 'in seeing these elegant erudites bring their highly complex and artificial method – the fruit of culture, and leisure, and luxury – to bear upon the crudities and maladies of life, and pick out choice morsels of available misery upon their gold pen-points.')

Margaret Oliphant's *A Beleaguered City* (1880) is a supernatural story set in France. It's one book, though a very special book, among the many which poured from her. She was prolific, and for hard-headed, practical reasons. She needed the money, for she had to support a family composed mainly of weak men. The American critic Elaine Showalter has commented on the troubles of Oliphant's working life: '[She] fought a never-ending battle against bankruptcy. The sole support of her own children, and [of] her nephews as well, she lived in perpetual bondage to a string of publishers, selling ideas for books she had not begun to write, and writing books she never cared for, simply to stay ahead. The British Museum has volumes of her letters to publishers, begging for an advance, or referring to a series of travel books, biographies, or text books that she was churning out.'

She developed a long-term working relationship with the Edinburgh publisher Blackwoods, but even so the flow of cheques from them wasn't always assured. On top of all this, she suffered many bereavements and other family problems. Her husband Frank was an artist, a designer of stained-glass windows, and died in his early forties when they were living in Rome. She became a widow at the age of 31. They had actually travelled to Rome for the sake of his health.

Frank had never earned as much as she did – she was always the breadwinner. Her brother Willie was an alcoholic, and another brother lost his job, came to live with her and brought his family along as well. She was always worried about her sons – they couldn't find jobs – and were lazy as well as not being in good health. Her sons predeceased her, and back in 1864, her daughter Maggie had died suddenly at the age of 10, in Rome.

In her *Autobiography* she records all this without self-pity. As someone who had been raised in the Free Presbyterian Church she was trained not to display her emotions. However, though she was tough, she was also vulnerable, and at times that is evident in the *Autobiography*. Here she is, writing in Albano, Italy, on 13th March 1864, six weeks after losing her daughter:

> So many burdens as I have, so much to do, so little help in this hard way of life, he [God] might have left me my little band of children unbroken [...]
>
> How He sows children broadcast about this world, how they swarm untaught,uncared for by the score in these Italian villages, living in beggary and wretchedness.
>
> Oh my Lord why didst Thou grudge to me the one blossom of womanhood I thought my own. (*The Autobiography of Margaret Oliphant*, edited and introduced by Elizabeth Jay, 1990, p. 9)

So even a devout Protestant lady, under emotional pressure, could cry out to God, why? why?

Margaret Oliphant's supernatural stories are very much concerned with bereavement, and how the living and the dead attempt to communicate with each other. *A Beleaguered City* is set in the town of Semur in Burgundy. The story unfolds during the early years of the Third French Republc, not long after the country's disastrous defeat in the Franco-Prussian War of 1870. In this novel there are many references to that war and its aftermath; it was of course an event of European as well as French significance. This has the effect of creating a context much wider than the provincial concerns of the people of Semur. War brings with it extreme experiences of death and bereavement, but premature death was a feature of nineteenth-century life in peace as well as in war, as Margaret Oliphant knew only too well. Fatal disease was rife, and children were especially susceptible.

In *A Beleaguered City*, the dead of Semur include children; they return to haunt their parents and relatives who are still living. Since 1859 and the publication of *The Origin of Species*, Darwin's theory of evolution challenged people's faith in the supposed certainties of religion, not least in Genesis and the story of Adam and Eve. Margaret Oliphant would never have been a crude creationist – she was too intelligent and sophisticated for that – but she distrusted Darwinism and the claims of science. That may not be surprising, given her religious background. However, she had her own special reasons for resisting such influences.

Scientific materialism just couldn't help people come to terms with the loss of their loved ones. In her introduction to the Oxford World Classics edition of *A Beleaguered City*, Merryn Williams suggests that tales of the supernatural were popular at this time because they posited a life beyond this one, and people needed to believe, desperately, that death wasn't the end, especially with the loss of so many at an early age. If we could make contact with the spirits of our dead children (and our dead adults), they could restore a spiritual meaning to life.

So for Margaret Oliphant to write ghost stories wasn't merely a matter of producing a popular, money-making type of fiction; it answered a profound existential need. Communication with our dead wouldn't bring them back, but parents especially would be assured that their children weren't completely lost to them.

Why 'beleaguered'? When the dead return to the Semur, a strange darkness settles on the town, and a strong wind drives its living inhabitants out of the town's gates. The supernatural events reach a climax at the cathedral, which is at the highest point of the town. During the early decades of the Third Republic, beginning in the 1870s, many French people had become sceptical of the teachings of the Catholic Church; however, Margaret Oliphant surmised that even those who still professed belief were in practice markedly materialistic, enjoying a comfortable bourgeois existence: the very pattern of narrow-minded, self-righteous provincialism. The return of the dead children, as well as of other dead relatives, challenges the smug materialism of the townsfolk, although it doesn't altogether overcome such attitudes. Moreover, Margaret Oliphant's real quarrel is with out-and-out materialism: in France and Europe generally the complacent belief in material progress was a major feature of that system of thought called Positivism. Such 'Progress', it was assumed, would inevitably lead to universal happiness. *A Beleaguered City* reflects the debate in France during the 1870s between those who broadly accepted the implications of Positivism, and those who yearned for more spiritual, religious values.

At the opposite extreme from Positivism was an attraction to mysticism (which would prove to be an ingredient of the determinedly anti-Positivistic Symbolist movement in the arts of France and beyond). In one of Oliphant's shorter supernatural tales, 'Old Lady Mary', there is a doctor who scoffs at a young woman's belief that she's been in contact with someone from 'the other side'. He says that all the woman needs is some medicine and all will be fine. The doctor displays the typical scientific-materialist denial of a spiritual dimension. In another story, 'The Land of Darkness', Oliphant offers us a picture of hell, a latter-day Dantesque inferno. She was much interested in Dante, and even wrote a book about him. However, the hell in her story resembles not so much an after-life as a dreadful science-fiction future, where human values have gone into decline in favour of an impersonal, technocratic dystopia, a kind of end-product of the Positivist outlook.

Yet *A Beleaguered City* isn't altogether a post-Dantean vision of eternal torment. After the initial terror is over, there is something enhancing coming out of the experience of the living people of Semur – they've made contact with those loved ones whom they'd lost. Still, neither is this a tale of sweet affirmation. There are folk who return to their simultaneous embrace of God and Mammon, to their cloying *mélange* of piety and avarice.

As an observant outsider, Margaret Oliphant has managed to convey much of the late nineteenth-century *Zeitgeist* of France, and indeed the late nineteenth-century *Zeitgeist* of much of Europe, in this short novel which was admired by a young Robert Louis Stevenson. *A Beleaguered City* reads like a 'French' novel with a distinct Scottish accent.

Patrick Geddes and the Call of the South

Back in the 1870s, when the polymath Patrick Geddes (1854-1932) still had a long way to go, his compatriot Robert Louis Stevenson was travelling with a donkey in the Cévennes. That region was not within what we'd call Mediterranean France, but RLS recalled that he spoke with folk 'who either pretended or believed that they had seen, from the Pic de Finiels, white ships sailing by Montpellier and Cette'. When Stevenson eventually made his way towards the coast, he wrote of 'the shock of wonder and delight' with which he found that he'd 'passed the indefinable line that separates South from North.'

It's debatable where that line continues to the east: I myself experienced it at Bergamo in northern Italy. There, the foothills of the Alps were before me, further north; in the other direction there stretched the plain of Lombardy, with promise of Venice and Naples far beyond. Others might cite a point even further north, in the Swiss city of Lucerne, whose Rathaus (town hall) has an Italianate Renaissance look about it; overall, though it's topped by a very Germanic roof. A building that's also a cultural frontier, as it were.

Stevenson headed to the Med for health reasons, but there was also the freedom from the Victorian Presbyterian gloom of his north. Later, the Scottish Colourist painters would make their way to such places as Cassis for that quality of light which was unavailable back home. Samuel Peploe's boss, in an Edinburgh lawyer's office, had warned him against a career in art, advising him that the 'divine afflatus' might turn out to be nothing more than 'wind in the stomach'.

There we have a collectible example of what poet Alan Bold called 'Scotland, the land of the Omnipotent No'! Undeterred, RLS and those of his and succeeding generations of young Scots found in the south of France a land of (for them) liberation. The painter J D Fergusson had a particular penchant for the sensuous in art and life; Charles Rennie Mackintosh discovered a last refuge at Port Vendres, which moved him to these strange, alluring watercolours which have you wondering, are they by the same man who designed the Glasgow School of Art building?

Stevenson goes on to describe how even a slightly different angle of vision or unexpected perspective can illuminate a Mediterranean scene for us in a new way; this can be occasioned by 'a change of posture or by those phenomena where even the colour is indeterminate and continually shifting, now you would say it was green, now grey, now blue; now tree stands above tree... massed into filmy indistinctness; and now, at the wind's will, the whole sea of foliage is shaken and broken up with little momentary silverings and shadows'. Surely this, again during the 1870s, anticipates Cézanne – that mentor (in effect) of the Scottish Colourists – and Cubism, which John Berger has called an art of interaction, in that it goes beyond the limitations of one single viewpoint in order to show the multifaceted, dialectical nature of the objective world.

Which is precisely what Geddes is all about: *interaction*, in what one would see from his Outlook Tower up Edinburgh's Old Town – Arthur's Seat (geology), St Giles' Cathedral (theology), the castle (history), the New Town far below (civics; horticulture; industry; commerce), the rural hinterland (agriculture). All these loci and their activities / intellectual disciplines work themselves out in necessary inter-relationships. 'Watertight compartments are of use', Geddes declared, 'only to a sinking ship.'

That concept of the Outlook Tower, first encountered by Geddes on his botanical-geological forays up Perth's Kinnoull Hill with its panorama of Fife and all the lands beyond it, finds its apotheosis atop the tower of the Scots College of Montpellier. It is vital that this structure be saved, given its centrality to Geddes's vision (one would say, in the light (the light!) of the foregoing, his *multi*-vision) and in the wider context of the geocultural polarities – West/East as well as North/South – that have featured so powerfully in the intellectual discourse of recent centuries.

Let's talk a bit more about these polarities. Geddes was not only a northerner looking south, but also a westerner looking east, most consummately in his work at Bombay and in his productive friendship with Rabindranath Tagore.

It was that staunch Italophile Goethe (also, significantly a west-to-east man) who, above all, introduced his fellow-northerners to that yearning for the polar Other: 'Kennst du das Land wo die

Zitronen blühn' – 'Do you know the land where the lemon-trees blossom'. More combatively, Nietzsche followed that up by his exaltation of Bizet's Hispanic opera *Carmen* over Wagner's ultra-Germanic *Ring*. Bizet, according to Nietzsche, had successfully 'mediterraneanised' music, and *Carmen* had a refreshing lightness about it – lightness as opposed to both darkness and heaviness of the Teutonic sort. That quality of Southern 'light' again, against Northern haar.

Take also Baudelaire, whose poetry at many points invokes 'le voyage' – escape from a Paris messed up by the authoritarian town-planning of Napoleon III's Second Empire, towards the infinity and eternity of the sea and that mystical Orient so beloved of nineteenth-century French artists in all media. (Geddes's eastern approaches were no less visionary, but a great deal more practical and grounded.) Mind you, Baudelaire's 'voyages' also included a passion for the further-north, for a land of Cockaigne much resembling the Netherlands, which might have been mist-ridden but also possessed a certain ambience of what could be summed up as *intimacy*. Not all north Europeans yearned exclusively for the south, and indeed the Austro- German poet Rilke, while based at Viareggio, actually felt a hankering for Scandinavia! And it was at Amalfi that Ibsen wrote that quintessentially intimate (though claustrophic) play of small-town Norway, *A Doll's House*, whose heroine Nora loves to dance the tarantella 'as if [her] life depended on it'. This north-south relationship seems constantly to caper back and forth, teasingly, flirtatiously.

In an essay on Melville's *Moby Dick*, the Mexican novelist Carlos Fuentes suggested that northern (Anglo-Saxon) peoples were spiritual on the surface but materialistic deep down, and that southern (Latin) peoples were materialistic on the surface but spiritual deep down. Be that as it may, Geddes's Montpellier tower accumulates considerable symbolic power.

Let's not be touristically-sentimental about this. The Mediterranean isn't all 'light'. It was at the Baumettes prison in Marseille that two of France's last executions, by guillotine, took place during the late 1970s. Behind the smart sets of Cannes and Antibes you have conurbations with grotty HLMs (*habitations à loyer modérés*), crime, anti-immigrant racism. Such inequalities are exploited and reinforced by Marine Le Pen's Front National. When I saw the far-Right's election posters in places like Marseille and Toulon, some twenty years ago, I looked at the pasty, crimped faces of the candidates and thought: so this is the master-race?

And much if not most of the Italian electorate seemed quite happy to have Silvio Berlusconi as its longest-serving PM. Wherever we are, north, south, west, east, we need all of Geddes's civilising force that we can get, and the Montpellier tower remains a testimony to that.

I'll end where I began, with RLS. Geddes admired Stevenson and it was his fellow-Scotsman's *The Strange Case of Dr Jekyll and Mr Hyde* which suggested to him the word *necrology*: science in the service of death, destruction, evil, as opposed to what it could achieve for the good of mankind. So far, so pious. But Geddes was more of a clued-up educator than Stevenson. There's something more than a little patronising, if well-meaning, in the Edimbourgeois Stevenson's account of an encounter with a well-read working man in Leven, Fife (possibly this took place in a wooded lane in what is now Letham Glen), as if the guy was a convenient poster-boy for enlightened Scottish attitudes to education.

In (northern) France, RLS met 'a workman-innkeeper' called Bazin, whom he admired for his self-culture; a not ungenerous attitude of Stevenson's, if still a bit *de haut en bas*, and continuing in this fashion: 'if anyone has read Zola's description of the workman's marriage party visiting the Louvre, they would do well to have heard Bazin by way of antidote.' Oh dear. RLS always relished the chance of a gratuitous swipe at Zola, whose unrelenting realism was so doucely rejected by the Scot. We're a long way, here, from the brave, anti-colonialist 'j'accuse' stance which Stevenson was to take in the south Pacific islands.

With his open, generalist philosophy – and practice – of education, at Montpellier and at his many other sites of activity, Geddes enriched the lives of many working folk and their families. He could have achieved even more if he'd been given the chance. Witness, say, his plans for a people's more-than-university in Dunfermline's Pittencrieff Park. Sure, Geddes could be a clumsily overwhelming figure, and he lacked RLS's elegant prose style, but more often than not he treated his students as co-equals in the quest for knowledge.

He offered, to borrow a phrase of the Scottish pianist-composer Ronald Stevenson, a certain 'hospitality of the mind'. Let's honour his legacy, preserve it, and (above all) act upon it!

Re-evaluation: R B Cunninghame Graham

'I valued Cunninghame Graham beyond rubies.' Thus wrote Hugh MacDiarmid of a man who performed a major role in embryonic stages of the Scottish Renaissance. The movement itself, as it gathered its youthful momentum, claimed the active interest of one who in his late seventies was still a striking figure on a platform, rallying his fellow Scots to the struggle for their nation's cultural and political identity.

The writing career of Robert Bontine Cunninghame Graham (1852-1936) belongs mainly to an earlier period, and the life and art of Scotland in those years between the 1880s and 1920s have still to receive their due. Graham's own work has been sadly neglected, even by those likely to be sympathetic to it, but the reasons for this can be readily understood. The Scottish Renaissance movement itself has come to overshadow the preceding generations against which much of its campaigning was directed. According to MacDiarmid, those generations failed to appreciate their best minds; Graham had to leave Scotland, which was deprived of a valuable self-corrective.

MacDiarmid claimed that Graham was driven into work other than that for which he was most urgently required. His subject-matter was drawn from all over the world, but very rarely from Scotland itself. It seemed that the nationalist activities of his old age, though prodigious, were a frantic making up for lost time.

At first sight there appears to be something patchy about Graham's achievement. One might well be tempted to categorise him neatly into apparently disparate roles (broadly corresponding to successive periods in his life) – the traveller and adventurer, the socialist and MP, the writer, the nationalist – and sum it all up by saying, well, he's an interesting minor figure, a talented eccentric, and no more. In fact a closer look at his work reveals a clearly unified pattern. The various strands come together and firmly intertwine: there emerges from the dusty wraps a rich and glowing tapestry, no mean banner for Scottish internationalism, that synthesis of apparent opposites.

Much of Graham's potential may have been lost, but the time for regrets is past. It is now much more worthwhile to examine him in a positive spirit, to discover those qualities which on many occasions moved MacDiarmid to enthusiastic tribute. Graham was one of those Scots, so often celebrated by MacDiarmid, who turned up in all parts of the globe. His manifold activities in Latin America, Spain and Africa are well documented both by himself and others, his own accounts (particularly *Mogreb-el-Acksa*, 1898) placing him in the front rank of writers of travel literature. This genre has a worthy Scottish tradition, in which Graham was preceded by Stevenson, another exile. Neither comfortable tourist nor rootless cosmopolitan, Graham was always ready to make perceptive comparisons between the problems of Scotland and of those lands which have since come under the heading 'Third World'. His experiences in the latter provided him with insights into the power and mentality of imperialism. One of his best stories, 'Al Hegira' (*Thirteen Stories* 1900), describes the escape of a group of Indian captives, six warriors, a woman and a boy. Their number diminishes in the course of an arduous and hazardous journey until the remnant is cornered by a Texan ranch owner whose brusque brutality is hardly redeemed by sentimental qualms: 'I hed a Winchester, and at the first fire tumbled the buck; he fell right in his tracks, and jest as I was taking off his scalp, I'm doggoned if the squaw and the young devil didn't come at us jest like grizzly bars. Wal yes, killed 'em o' course, and anyhow the young un would have growed up, but the squaw I'me sort of sorry about, I never could bear to kill a squaw, though I've often seen it done'. In a letter as early as 1879, Graham had commented ironically on the righteousness evoked when the oppressed fought back. 'Why is it both in England & America when white troops win it is a victory & when beaten, it is termed a horrible massacre. I always thought a massacre meant when the massacred could not resist'. The lessons of Scotland's own history of violence and degradation could not be lost on a man like Graham.

His term for British Zimbabwe was 'Fraudesia', but whereas many Liberals were prepared to support the Boers against the British in South Africa, Graham denounced both sides. In 1896 appeared his pamphlet *The Imperial Kailyard*. Graham's identification of other subject nations with his own is evident in the title's reference to the 'Kailyard' school of writers, whose one-sided, lachrymose view of Scotland appealed to the English and to the Scots themselves. Graham's pamphlet ends with a passionate denunciation of the vulgarity, brutality and false consciousness engendered by the

Empire both overseas and within Britain itself:

> No one doubts that eventually the Matabele will be conquered, and that our flag will wave triumphantly over the remnant of them in the same way as it waves triumphantly over the workhouse pauper and the sailors' poor whore in the east end of London. Let it wave on over an empire reaching from north to south, from east to west, wave over every island, hitherto ungrabbed, on every sterile desert and fever-haunted swamp as yet unclaimed; over the sealer amid the icebergs, stripping the fur from the live seal, on purpose to oblige a lady; over the abandoned transport camel, perishing of thirst in the Soudan: and still keep waving over Leicester Square, where music halls at night belch out crowds of stout imperialists.

Between the years 1886 and 1892 Graham was a *de jure* Liberal but *de facto* socialist Member of Parliament. The citizen of the world was well equipped to campaign both in and out of the House – an 'Asylum for Incapables' he called it – for a wide range of causes. The less far-flung of his concerns included the miners of his Lanarkshire constituency. His developing commitment to Scottish Home Rule was strengthened by his interest in Ireland, for which he was arrested during the 'Bloody Sunday' riot of November 1887 and sentenced to six weeks in Pentonville (His experiences of prison life led to the fine essay, 'Sursum Corda' (*Success*, 1902)). In the history of the left in Britain at the close of the century Graham ranks with his friends William Morris and Keir Hardie; he described their funerals movingly in 'With the North-West Wind (*The Ipané*, 1899) and 'With the North-East Wind' (*Brought Forward*, 1916). A fervent admirer of Graham was Engels, who wrote to Marx's daughter Laura: 'So we are represented in the British Parliament too'. Engels even described him as 'Marxian', something denied by MacDiarmid, who regretted that Graham had 'not gone all out from the beginning for Scottish workers' republicanism à la John Maclean'. Graham was certainly wanting in firm theoretical foundations. In August 1914, against the expectations of his comrades, and unlike John Maclean, Graham abandoned the anti-war line. For him, the international workers' movement took second place to the fight against what he considered German barbarism. The following years were his period of serious political inconsistency. Having earlier dismissed the Liberals as 'crutch-and-toothpick gentlemen', believing them to be ideologically two-faced, he stood for West Stirling in 1918 – as a Liberal. One of the less edifying features of his campaign was his taste for fatuous jokes against the pacifism of his Labour opponent.

Many will find his conduct at this time difficult to excuse, but it can be explained. He was impulsive and idiosyncratic, qualities that were his weakness as well as his strength. Disillusionment made him politically isolated and insecure. The conservatism of the mass of the workers became a source of great frustration, as he made clear in a review (*Clarion*, 12th September 1902) of a book by Robert Blatchford. Other leftist writers certainly felt likewise, notably Blatchford himself, and Robert Tressell in his novel *The Ragged Trousered Philanthropists*. Furthermore, Graham detected incipient careerism among the 'p[iss] pot Socialists' of the Labour Party. He also despised the petty-minded puritanism of the left as much as that of the Nonconformist Liberals, writing drily of 'the happy time when all shall sit, apparelled in one livery, at little tables, drinking some kind of not too diuretic 'table water' approved by the County Council, and reading expurgated Bibles'. Graham needed something nobler, life-affirming, as an alternative to a capitalist civilisation 'founded on mud, cemented with blood, sustained precariously upon the points of bayonets.'

A lesser man would have defected totally to the enemy, to become like one of those trendy righties so ubiquitous in our own time. However, his political resurrection came in the 1920s with his most explicit and sustained involvement in the Scottish cause; he eventually became the first President of the National Party of Scotland. Late in the day as all this was (and it was late in the day for everyone else), it was the logical result of his life-long radical response to a variety of societies and cultures, a response always strongest when a Scottish dimension was present. Home Rule had been for him 'the first step to internationalism, the goal which every thinking man and woman must place before their eyes'. In a speech in Glasgow in 1887 he had won cheers for his remarks on 'the spirit of national independence, without which man indeed, even a Scotchman, is but a tinkling bagpipe'.

This was not the talk of a narrow, parochial 'Scots-wha hae' verer'. His pamphlet. *Self Government for Scotland* is the transcript of a speech delivered at Elderslie in 1920 on the 615th anniversary of Sir William Wallace's execution. Here he refused to restrict Wallace's significance to Scotland alone and claimed that he shared world stature with other national heroes such as Garibaldi, Mazzini and Bolivar. He argued that Wallace was an internationalist ahead of his time, citing his letter to the Hanseatic League which called on them:

> To afford protection to certain Scottish merchants who were going to Bremen, Lubeck and Hamburg to trade, and promising protection to the merchants of the Hanseatic League, when their mercantile affairs should bring them to Scotland. If they [Graham's audience] read the records of any other countries of that time, notably those of the Genoese and Venetian Republics and many others shortly after they were instituted, they would find a widely different spirit to that which animated the national hero of Scotland. Nearly everyone of those other Republics cut themselves off by impenetrable walls of protection – by arms, by tariffs, and by customs – in order that their merchants should be protected: but Wallace understood clearly that there could be no international goodwill without international reciprocity and protection to the merchants of the various nationalities.

It was characteristic that Graham should in this speech pay tribute to other small nations such as Czechoslovakia and Poland, which were more actively conscious of their identities than Scotland. Graham was impressed by the outburst of Polish patriotism which his close friend Joseph Conrad permitted himself in his tale of 1911, 'Prince Roman'. Conrad described fashionable anti-nationalism in terms of its 'vulgar refinement', on which quality Graham commented: 'We are suffocated with it'. Graham went on: 'Poland indeed, in 1911, was the Cinderella of the nations, sitting amongst the ashes, outraged, mocked at and oppressed and crucified between the three great empires who with their seal held her in servitude. He [Conrad] lived to see her free and take her place again amongst the nations of the world'. (Preface to Conrad's *Tales of Hearsay and Last Essays*, 1928). There seems to be an implied message here for Scotland. Seventy years after 'Prince Roman', Poland hardly needs to have it spelled out.

He was no more a Scottish Nationalist hack than he was a

Liberal or Labour hack. MacDiarmid remarked that Graham and Compton Mackenzie 'in council with the officials and branch delegates of the Scottish Nationalist Party were like a pair of golden eagles, with their wings clipped, in a crowded poultry-run, full of poultry far gone with the 'gapes''. More than most self-styled Scottish Nationalists then and today [1981-82], he had a perspective on cultural values, seeking authentic ones to replace the conventional.

What was this perspective? As ever, his travels were a strong influence, but the fact that he was of both Scottish and Spanish ancestry had always been an advantage. Neil Munro believed that Graham's knowledge of Spanish greatly enriched his English prose style, especially in rhythm and unexpectedness. Graham actually wrote a number of pieces in Spanish, and was a prolific publicist of Spanish and Latin American life and literature in such prominent periodicals as the *Nation* and the *Saturday Review*. One could often find him championing Cervantes. In one review he took Unamuno to task. Here he is, in 1915, commending a book on a continent he knew so well:

> The chapter on the literature of the South Americas is illuminating, and will no doubt astonish many who probably have thought that such a thing as literature was non-existent in lands of 'saladeros', colossal fortunes, trackless forests and populations steeped in ignorance. Writers there are by scores, especially in Bogota, which may be called the Athens of Spanish America. In that favoured city poets abound, and he who does not write is as distinguished by his singularity as a man without a military title of some sort between the 'corn-belts' and the Pacific slope.

By contrast, when he had turned to what passed for Scottish literature in the 1890s he had denounced 'those awful McCrocketts and Larens' who had encouraged the image of a Scotsman as 'a sentimental fool, a canting cheat, a grave, sententious man, dressed in a 'stan o' black', oppressed with the tremendous difficulties of the jargon he is bound to speak, and above all weighed down with the responsibility of being Scotch'. In the essay 'A Survival (*The Ipané*) Graham anticipated later critics of the Kailyard such as George Douglas Brown, author of *The House with the Green Shutters*, and of course MacDiarmid. He believed that Scotland had been spiritually diminished by Calvinism and commerce. However, he was not content with a merely negative response to a negative mentality. He had more to offer than abuse, and maintained that Scotland had known greatness in 'pre-Knoxian and pre-bawbee days.' His estate was in Menteith, on the frontier of the Highlands and Lowlands, and he was conscious of the heroism and creativity of Gaeldom's past. He was a frequent contributor to a journal which sought to revive interest in this culture, *Guth na Bliadhna*. Much 'Celtic' enthusiasm at the turn of the century was almost alternative Kailyard, fashionably wistful and rarefied, as exemplified in the work of Fiona Macleod (William Sharp). Graham was a romantic, but a tough-minded one. Man needed bread, he wrote in 1913, as well as Brian Boru. His nationalism was still firmly underpinned by his socialism. He would lovingly evoke the mists of Menteith but he would not lose himself in them. 'In all his writing,' declared MacDiarmid, 'Cunninghame Graham belonged not to the Celtic Twilight but to the Gaelic sunshine'.

When he harked back to the primitive societies of the historically distant past and the geographically distant present, he was not unaware of their brutal side; he simply pointed out that at least they were more open about it than the agents of nineteenth-century industrialism and colonialism. His distaste for modern gimcrack civilisation would not have allowed him to adopt glibly the conventional Marxist position against the 'idiocy of rural life' but he was more than just the kind of 'aristocratic socialist' mocked by Marx and Engels in *The Communist Manifesto*. As the bitter sketch 'Salvagia' reveals, Graham was far from idealising the degraded Scottish peasantry. The fad for Tolstoyan communes seems not to have affected him; he was too sophisticated to take refuge in illusory reactions. At the same time, he was never blasé, but possessed of a boundless curiosity not just for the intellectual, but also for the instinctive. He felt that pre-industrial peoples, though under threat, still lived in harmony with elemental forces. Graham can be usefully compared with a later foreign interpreter of the Latin American scene, the enigmatic B Traven. Both celebrated a sensuous – even pagan – joy in living, in creativity, and in nature (Chapter 6 of Graham's *Notes on the District of Menteith*, 1895, is headed 'Pantheistic'). Modern society had repressed this in the pursuit of piety and profit – 'men begin at twenty to enter nothings in a ledger' – and it was something that had to be rediscovered in changed circumstances. This was what Graham's and Traven's politics and art were driving at.

Graham's interest in Scottish writers such as Dunbar and Henryson may also be part of the pattern of relating a better past to a better future. It suggests a sense that Scotland once possessed a European outlook and still had the potential to develop an outlook that was even more than European. Graham made his own contribution to Scottish literature in an internationalist spirit. His very choice of form – the short story – reveals this. He felt that long, diffuse novels had become the preserve of the Anglo-Saxons and Teutons; the Latins preferred to be concise. He once berated a *Saturday Review* critic for using the phrase 'only a short story'. Such condescension showed how much writers in England were 'out of touch with the trend of literature in those benighted portions of the world outside the sweet influence of the Brixton Pleiades'. If this seems an oversimplification we can turn to his enthusiastic preface to a translation of Maupassant's stories: 'To his Latin clarity and ruthless logic, Maupassant joins what the generality of Latins (except the Spaniards) often lack, the gift of humour. But, then he was a Norman, allied on that side of his mentality to the English, or perhaps nearer to the Scotch.' In such tales as, say, 'Rothenberger's Wedding' (*Thirteen Stories*), Graham has Maupassant's knack of a clear plot-line that turns on some matter of deft irony. Perhaps this is what attracted him to translate Santiago Rusiñol's short play *La Verge de Mar*, in which some villagers come across a wooden figure cast up by the sea. They believe it to be a statue of the Virgin and worship it It gets the credit for some local miracles. However, one of the subsequent pilgrims is a sea-captain who recognises that the statue is his ship's figurehead, representing not the Virgin but his Moslem mistress. He is asked not to reveal the truth to the villagers. Graham's version, from the Catalan, has apparently been performed only once, at the Maddermarket Theatre, Norwich, in 1958. A revival at the Edinburgh Fringe would be ideal.

The subject matter of Graham's stories also often recalls Maupassant but comes naturally from his social concerns. He writes of outcasts and exiles with commitment but never with solemnity. In one story we came across a crazed political idealist, in another a respectable prostitute. A black poet is fêted by white society as an artist but rejected as a man in 'Mirahuano' (*Hope*,

1910, reprinted in *The Penguin Book of Scottish Short Stories*, edited by J F Hendry). Graham's opposition to the exploitation of women is powerfully evident in the tragic 'A Wire-Walker' (*His People*, 1906). So many of Graham's pieces are on the borderline between story and sketch. In these instances he seems closer to Chekhov than to Maupassant; plot becomes of less importance than mood, Chekhov's *nastroenie*, of which Graham offers us a Scottish equivalent. In 1925 MacDiarmid referred to Graham as one of the six best short story writers which Scotland had yet produced.

Graham was keenly interested in the visual arts, and appears to have felt that here at least contemporary Scotland was being adventurous, drawing her inspiration 'from Paris rather than from Hampstead'. John Lavery and Joseph Crawhall, of the Glasgow School of painters, were his friends; William Strang, another Scot, used him as the model for his illustrations to *Don Quixote*. William Rothenstein and Jacob Epstein were also close. As chairman of the W H Hudson Memorial Committee, Graham commissioned Epstein to produce an appropriate tribute to the Anglo-Argentinian writer and naturalist. The avant-garde bas-relief depicted the girl Rima, the embodiment of Nature in Hudson's *Green Mansions*, in glorious nakedness; after unveiling the monument in Hyde Park, Prime Minister Baldwin was seen to shudder. There was an outcry in the English press, but Graham and his supporters fought back with relish, and the monument remains near the spot where Hudson used to sleep rough in his early, obscure days in London. This was not Graham's first campaign against insularity in the visual arts: he had earlier taken up the cudgels on behalf of the Post-Impressionists.

The well-paid pessimists of the United Kingdom of South-East England have not been slow to simper at the name of Cunninghame Graham. Malcolm Muggeridge – of all people – dismissed him as a poseur. Unfortunately most discussion of Graham has concentrated on his life rather than on his work, and has encouraged the image of a narcissist and dilettante, as if this writer of impressionistic prose was his own masterpiece of impressionism. The personality cult of 'Don Roberto' has harmed Graham just as that of 'RLS' harmed Stevenson. Worst of all, he has been called a cynic; he was certainly a sceptic, as Conrad observed, but that did not diminish him as an active idealist. It was said of him in 1888 that he was 'a man with a mission, and languid

London does not love men with missions'. Graham himself. late in life, put it thus:

> I believe, and it is good for man to believe in something fervently, even in Voodoo, that intense vitality is of itself a kind of genius. Genius I mean for life, for most men hardly ever are alive, passing from golf to tennis, and ending up with bridge, till they ascend to join in singing 'Rule Britannia' in the heavenly choirs.

Hugh MacDiarmid: The Integrative Vision

Baudelaire, Rilke, MacDiarmid: these are modern poets who have resisted the fragmenting, trivialising tendencies of their times. All three share a universality of outlook. Baudelaire held that God had created an indivisible unity, 'dark and profound'; accordingly, the human senses (and therefore the arts) were inter-related – they 'corresponded' to each other. Cooks and perfumers were artists as much as painters, composers and poets. Truly great artists were those who did not specialise narrowly in one activity, who had a deep and broad culture. On their canvasses, colour became melody. In particular, Baudelaire cited Delacroix, a painter with an intense appreciation of poetry and music, a visionary genius in contrast to the fashionable triflers of the Second Empire.

Rilke rejected Baudelaire's Christian God; poetry itself was the goal of his spirituality. He learned, though, that poetry also required materiality. This was the lesson of sculpture. Rilke became secretary to Rodin, and in the master's studio he discovered how each sculpted hand, head, torso, could actually suggest the animation of a complete body. Each part was in itself a coherent whole. What was a fragment in life was no mere fragment in art. Moreover, in a group such as *The Burghers of Calais* (1884-89), each figure was both uniquely individual and an integral part of the group. This coherence was all the more remarkable in that none of the figures actually touched each other. For Rilke, Rodin was an artist who broke down reality then recomposed it into *'neue Verbindungen'* (new combinations). MacDiarmid called on his fellow artists to join him in 'binding the braids' – he takes the image from a Sanskrit text, but it almost echoes Rilke's German phrase.

Rilke, as consummate an art-critic/poet as Baudelaire, learned from Rodin how to overcome writer's block: in a sense he replaced it with sculptor's block, the block to which the sculptor addresses himself every day in his workmanlike fashion, unlike the poet waiting pathetically for 'inspiration'. In his *'Dinggedicht'* – 'thing' poems – Rilke approached his subject matter with the maximum attention, having examined it from all angles, having humbly and patiently allowed it to yield its essence to him – just like Rodin. Art, then, is the supreme integrator, not least when it integrates the verbal and the visual.

MacDiarmid's integrative vision owes much to his native Langholm, a weaving town where three rivers meet. In 'The Seamless Garment', set among the Langholm looms, he praises Rilke as a poet who wove together his love and pity and fear into a 'seamless garment o music an thocht'. One of MacDiarmid's finest poems in English is his transcreation of Rilke's 'Requiem for the painter Paula Modersohn-Becker'.

In his rediscovery of the potentialities of the Scots language, MacDiarmid effectively applied Baudelaire's 'correspondences'. Scots, so rich in onomatopoeia, could evoke a wide range of sounds; he went further and claimed its potential for colours and smells. It is not surprising to find MacDiarmid writing a poem about music in terms of painting – 'Sibelius's gaunt El-Greco-emaciated ecstatic Fourth ('Goodbye Twilight') – or about painting in terms of music: the art of his fellow Borderer, William Johnstone, is related to Mahler's Eighth.

MacDiarmid's art appeals to ear and eye – indeed, it fulfils his ideal of a poetry of the whole person. We can cite the musicality of the early Scots lyrics, forby the surreal footage of *A Drunk Man Looks at the Thistle* :

Plant, what are you then? Your leafs
Mind me o the pipes' lood drone
– And a' your purple tops
Are the pirly-wirly notes
That gang staggerin owre them as they groan...

A Drunk Man illustrates Baudelaire's '*le beau est toujours bizarre*'; eleven years after that pronouncement, Aeneas Sweetland Dallas maintained that 'you cannot have great art which is not weird'. In drawing attention to Dallas's *The Gay Science* (1866), MacDiarmid was rediscovering one of these Scots (or at least semi-Scots) who were precursors of the continental Europeans – in this case Freud and Jung. MacDiarmid's *Aesthetics in Scotland* is a journey through Scottish visual art in quest of a Scottish aesthetic, and here Dallas is revealed as a pioneer who considered art in relation to symbolism and the unconscious rather than to Victorian morality.

Rilke's most celebrated '*Dinggedicht*', 'The Panther', is concerned with vision and the relation between observer and observed. The Great Wheel section of *A Drunk Man* has been praised for its scientific insight

Oor universe is like an e'e
Turned in, man's benmaist hert to see,
And swamped in subjectivity…

The protagonist of *A Drunk Man* speculates that man may evolve faculties by which he will fuse subjectivity and objectivity:

The function, as it seems to me,
O' Poetry is to bring to be
At lang, lang last that unity…

MacDiarmid, as appropriate for a twentieth-century poet, goes further than Baudelaire and Rilke in integrating poetry with science. His ally William McCance called for the visual arts to do likewise, writing that the Scots, with their ability for construction and engineering, need not tolerate sentimentality in their art. MacDiarmid corroborated by pointing out that in the past there had been two factors, man and nature, now there was a third, the machine. (MacDiarmid's relations with Johnstone and McCance, are explored in Duncan MacMillan's *Scottish Art 1460-1990*).

Two more MacDiarmid texts remain to be cited in connection with the verbal and the visual. The first is *The Kind of Poetry I Want*, ie, the kind of poetry which learns from the visual arts, a poetry as subtle and complete and tight as the 'integration of the thousands of brush strokes/ In a Cézanne canvas': exactly that quality which Rilke found in the composition of a portrait of Mme Cézanne: 'It seems that each part knows of all the other parts' (letter to Clara Rilke, 22nd October 1907).

Secondly, there is 'A Glass of Pure Water', with its near-Rilkean figure of an Angel reporting on a hundred years of human life by means of a single, subtle gesture of the hand. Rilke himself, through his fictional mouthpiece Malte Laurids Brigge, maintained that a poem's existence depended on 'glance and gesture'. A tacit recognition of this might be found in Scotland's poetry-theatre movement.

In Memoriam James Joyce is MacDiarmid's most explicit and exuberant statement of his integrative vision. He considered his poem to be 'ablaze with the sense that we stand at one of the great turning points of human history… a complete breakdown of civilisation is possible and can only be averted if we can succeed in unifying mankind at a high level of culture'. He stresses unity-in-diversity: the world's various language-cultures are enriched by mutual respect and creative reciprocity:

> And rejoicing in all those intranational differences which
> Each like a flower's scent by its peculiarity sharpens
> Appreciation of others as well as bringing
> Appreciation of itself, as experiences of gardenia or zinnia
> Refine our experience of rose or sweet pea.

The poet defended the 'multiplicity of quotations, references and allusions' in his poem by invoking Baudelaire's 'immense clavier des correspondances'. The clavier image is apt for *In Memoriam*, which tends to allude more to music than to the visual arts; indeed, one of the most suggestive essays on the poem is by a composer-pianist, Ronald Stevenson (in *Hugh MacDiarmid: a Festschrift*, Edinburgh, 1962). In the 'Plaited like the Generations of Men' section, MacDiarmid transcribes into poetry an essay by the composer-pianist Busoni – himself an avid transcriber of other composers, notably Bach.

I'll conclude with one portion of the Busoni-MacDiarmid transcription. This passage also serves as 'A Point in Time', MacDiarmid's poetic response to Johnstone's painting of that name: it hangs in the Scottish National Gallery of Modern Art, and is a key work in twentieth-century Scottish painting. It is movingly appropriate that all the arts should come together in this most celestial-terrestrial of MacDiarmid's utterances of integration:

> Now you understand how stars and hearts are one with another
> And how there can nowhere be an end, nowhere a hindrance;
> How the boundless dwells perfect and undivided in the spirit,
> How each part can be at once infinitely great and infinitely small,
> How the utmost extension is but a point, and how
> Light, harmony, movenient, power
> All identical, all separate, and all united are life.

From Montsou to Bowhill:
Joe Corrie's Antecedents

Around 1994/5 my wife and I went to the Adam Smith Theatre in Kirkcaldy to see a screening of Claude Berri's movie *Germinal*, based on Emile Zola's novel of that name, and set in the coalfields of northern France. In the queue as we waited to be admitted were a number of guys who had worked down the Fife pits.

Joe Corrie has often been likened to the Zola of *Germinal*, not least by my good friend Willie Hershaw, and also to D H Lawrence, whose dad had been a Nottinghamshire miner. In the course of this talk, I want to say something about how Corrie actually differs from Zola and Lawrence. Hopefully a comparative approach may help to illuminate anew certain of Corrie's qualities.

Zola's *Germinal* was published in 1885, though the action of the novel takes place some two decades earlier, during the Second French Empire régime of Napoléon III, a vulgar and meretricious period during which the rich got ostentatiously richer and the poor got less ostentatiously poorer, though things were hardly better in 1885 during the Third Republic. Zola himself was, as they say, humbly born, and could empathise naturally with the miners whom he was writing about while not being a miner himself. When he visited the northern French coalfields to research the novel, he took copious notes – copious note-taking was integral to his literary method, as he espoused the doctrine of Naturalism, a more intense form of Realism based very self-consciously on purportedly scientific enquiry. Zola was aiming to write what he called 'experimental' novels, as if he were in a laboratory observing how his fictional characters interacted with each other, as if they were test-tube specimens. This creed stressed the influence of heredity and environment on human behaviour, and this tended to be naïvely deterministic – there's an inexorability about the course of his characters' lives. This must be distinguished from the not dissimilar sense we get from reading Thomas Hardy's novels; his characters are subject rather to portentously mystical forces – summed up as 'the President of the Immortals' – a late Victorian hangover, if you like, of the modes of Greek tragedy, and quite other than the non-theistic, philosophically materialist pretentions of Zola's method. All, all of this is a long way from the dynamics of Joe Corrie's plays and poems.

The character in *Germinal* through whom we witness most of the action in Zola's novel – the book's 'vessel of consciousness' to borrow a term of Henry James's – is Etienne Lantier. Like Zola himself, he's an outsider, who has headed north to work in the pits. Lantier arrives in the mining village of Montsou where the main pit is called Le Voreu. The Welsh writer Merryn Williams, in her study of *Germinal*, tells us that the name 'Le Voreu' suggests to her 'voracious', and indeed Zola evokes the pit with a grim poetry, as a monster which devours people. Indeed Zola has a powerfully poetic imagination which thankfully transcends his pseudo-scientific intentions.

Etienne Lantier the outsider struggles to communicate with his workmates – in Fife we'd call them 'neibours' [neighbours] – in the sense that he tries to imbue them with political consciousness. Their concerns, though, are so basic and immediate that his efforts don't work out. However, Lantier's own political consciousness is not quite adequate: he's read his Marx and his Darwin, but the ideas he has derived from them are half-baked – and half-baked intellectual food tends to be indigestible.

Moreover – and this applies to Zola himself as much as to Lantier – Darwin rather cancels out Marx. Zola's theories of literary Naturalism, with their stress on heredity and environment as determining human behaviour, are heavily influenced by Darwin. Humans are animals and the evolution of animal life proceeds by forces beyond the control of animals as a species or as individual specimens. Etienne Lantier, we learn, comes from a family with drink problems; his hereditary alcoholism, should he take a single drop, leads him to become violent. Environment is changeable; heredity you're stuck with. Darwinesque Naturalism is in effect a kind of secular Calvinism. You're predestined, you have no free will. True, interpretations of Marx have all too often ended up with economic determinism, but Marx is supposed to be about political action, and that implies free will. Actually, of all philosophers, Marx perhaps came closest to resolving the free will versus determinism debate when he wrote that 'Men make their own history, but they do not make it just as they please; they do not make it under circumstances chosen by themselves, but under circumstances directly encountered, given, and transmitted from the past.' OK, that still sounds like a tilt towards the determinism side, but, even so, the opening phrase holds: 'Men make their own history.'

Come to Joe Corrie's work, and Zolaism appears to be so much French theoretical baggage beside Scottish practical good sense, Fife practical good sense. Corrie was a committed socialist, and socialist values, socialist ethics, pervade his plays and his poetry; there is bitter indictment of the ruling class, the bosses; there are strikes. In the play *Hewers of Coal*, and in the poem 'Women Are Waiting Tonight', there's a pit disaster, with the subsequent crocodile tears of the bourgeoisie flowing as copiously as they do in *Germinal*; even so, in Corrie we have the sense of a community that describes and conducts itself on its own terms, as far as it can under what Marx would call the 'given circumstances'.

Corrie refuses to ascribe such circumstances to any kind of determinism, mystical or otherwise. To the politically committed, there is no inevitability about the possibly dire outcomes of economic and social flux. Corrie would have scorned the Tories' 1980s mantra of 'there is no alternative' to monetarism. His sonnet 'Oor Jean', about the victimisation of a strike leader, has these closing lines:

Some ca' this Fate that comes by God's decree;
Then God must be the Fife Coal Company.

The Marxist critic György Lukács called Zola a 'naïve liberal' and accused him of turning the 'socially pathological' into the 'psychopathological', while at the same time praising his courage in defending the scapegoated Jewish army captain at the centre of the Dreyfus Affair – the occasion for Zola's famously bold public letter 'J'accuse' levelled at the French Establishment and its anti-semitism, which would return even more horrifically fifty years later, as instigated by Marshal Pétain's far-right collaborationist Vichy régime.

Beside all this, the experience of the Fife pits might seem tame, as if Victor Hugo was correct when he remarked that the French want a full-scale revolution, while the English – and by extension the Scots? – opt rather for a well-behaved earthquake. But life in the Fife coalfields was more than grim enough, especially during the 1920s with the General Strike and the lock-out, during which my forebears among so many others suffered real deprivation. And the 'earthquakes' – the pit disasters – continued well into living memory, particularly in 1957 and 1967, respectively at the Lindsay and Michael pits. In Scottish poetry such tragedies have been recorded by T S Law in his *Licht Attoore the Face* and in Willie Hershaw's 'High Valleyfield'. I fell into the trap there of using such words as 'disasters' and 'tragedies', words which would reinforce the notion of the fault being in our stars, or in Greek-style Fate, such cop-outs as are challenged by Joe Corrie.

What is so striking about Joe Corrie when compared with his antecedents is his depiction of the lively folk culture of the Fife miners and their families. In *Germinal* the people of Montsou enjoy a certain respite when it's the time of the fair – the *ducasse*: Zola uses a northern French dialect word, roughly equivalent to the 'kermesse' of neighbouring Flanders. But it's not a verbal culture. Their Fife counterparts cherish and perform their Scottish folk songs and folk poetry, and – crucially – their Robert Burns: this indigenous culture features strongly in Corrie's plays. Traditionally the Scottish working class has been highly literate, with its culture of miners' and mechanics' institutes, evening classes, its working-folk's libraries and lectures, its collective self-education, and the more recent offshoots such as the WEA, the Workers' Educational Association. It was a Cowdenbeath miner's daughter, Jennie Lee, who founded the Open University.

An aside: there was a Scottish mining novel published in 1887, just a couple of years after *Germinal*. It's called *Blawearie*, subtitled 'Mining Life in the Lothians', and is by Peter McNeill. It has no great literary value, but it has interest as a social-historical document. At one point, the miners are talking about one of their new overseers, who has crossed the Firth of Forth to work in the Lothian pits. One of the guys remarks, 'he'll be awful cunning, for a' the Fifers are burstin' fu' o' that commodity.' Who am I to contradict that? Fly Fifers indeed.

OK, a miner's daughter, as I said, was founder of the OU, as Minister of the Arts in Harold Wilson's government, and a fly Fifer into the bargain. The miner's son D H Lawrence was a contemporary of Joe Corrie. In 1930 his essay 'Nottingham and the Mining Countryside' was published; there he wrote as follows:

The great crime which the moneyed classes and promoters

of industry committed in the palmy Victorian days was the
condemning of the workers to ugliness [...] The human soul
needs actual beauty even more than bread.

This takes us to one advantage that Corrie's miners had over
those who feature in Zola's and Lawrence's writings. The coalfields
of France and Nottinghamshire were drab, even if the latter had its
pockets of gentle rural relief, as in *Sons and Lovers*, with its bluebell
wood, sunset on hills, a blue lake. In Corrie's work, however,
there's a much greater celebration of more dramatic vistas, of the
expansive natural beauty just north of the central Fife pits – the
great hills of Benarty and the Lomonds. The means of escape
were within sight of Bowhill, Lochgelly, and the neighbouring pit
towns.

Moreover, that indigenous culture which I spoke of was not so
present in Nottinghamshire, if Lawrence is anything to go by. In
the early chapters of *Sons and Lovers* there's the odd snatch of a folk
poem about Adam and Eve; the miners 'rolling dismally home'
from the pub, pissed and sentimental, singing the hymn 'Lead,
kindly Light'.

Himself a playwright, Lawrence is in that sense the predecessor
of Corrie in representing miners' families on the stage. However,
any literary culture of any substance comes from the outside, it's
imported, and that awkwardly. Take Lawrence's best-known play,
A Collier's Friday Night, dating from around 1909, and which, like
the movie *Germinal*, we went to see in the Adam Smith Theatre in
Kirkcaldy, back in 1979. Again, the Lawrence piece would have
appealed to us in what was then still a mining town – though
Thatcherisation wasn't a long way off in the future. In his book
D H Lawrence: Life into Art, Keith Sagar informs us that the title
of Lawrence's play, *A Collier's Friday Night*, is an 'ironic allusion to
Burns's sentimental 'The Cotter's Saturday Night'.' It's telling that
Corrie wrote a play called *The Miner's Saturday Night*.

Yet without a Burns, what do the Lambert family in Lawrence's
play rely on for a literary culture? Well, as I said, on an external
literary culture. The college-educated lad Ernest is sitting near
his dour old man, who's relaxing after his shift down t'pit. Young
Ernest, who has acquired a certain affected way of speech, says to
his dad: 'Give me a bit of my paper, Father. You know the leaf I
want: that with the reviews of books on.' His old man replies: 'Nay,

I know nowt about reviews o' books. Here, t'art. Ta'e it.' Ernest's head is full of Swinburne and Baudelaire. I couldn't help but think of the Monty Python parody of this kind of scenario – where the rough old dad is a successful playwright, but the effete son prefers to be a miner. The old man, played by Graham Chapman, challenges the young one, played by Eric Idle: 'Oooo, ye want to go down t'pit, lad, eh? Being a West-End playwright isn't good enough for thee... oooo!'

Lawrence himself detested la-di-da Oxfordy literary pretentiousness, and he has some hilarious poems which satirise just that. In one of them, a smugly over-refined young man winds up a 'woman rather older than himself' to the point where she's had enough and she threatens to pull off her knickers in public. Actually, Joe Corrie takes great delight in mocking what he regards as those 'airy-fairy' poets who over-intellectualise. Their productions will be 'anaemic, flabby things, / Like pampered children from a wealthy home'. The speaker in one of his sonnets has regretted studying too much; he had decided to 'throw [his] bulky books away' and instead 'singing, went among my fellow-men'. Corrie denounced what he called 'The Modern Scots Poets' who ignored working-class folk: 'Poets in plenty, fu' o' self-esteem / Wi' odes as trifling as a tinker's fart.'

I think Corrie has a valid point, to put it mildly. His own poetry is simple and direct, and possesses the qualities of folk poetry, such as in those lines of his that impress themselves on the memory, and there's the sense you get in many of his poems that they seem to have composed themselves. He's a true heir of Burns. I remember the composer Ronald Stevenson remarking that the best poems to set to music are uncomplicated lyrics: abstruse poetry is unsuitable for such treatment. I'd say that there are exceptions – such an intricately cryptic poet like Rilke has been set successfully to music by the likes of Hindemith – but in evidence of the general point I'd draw your attention to the CD 'The Joe Corrie Project' recorded by the present-day Bowhill Players, that's to say Willie Hershaw and his fellow musicians, where you can hear Corrie's poems fitted naturally to powerful tunes.

Donald Campbell has written that 'Joe Corrie did not write for an audience that attended first nights in evening dress – as many did in those days – nor did he expect his plays to be the subject of university seminars.' Of course, the denunciation of 'difficult' poetry can go too far, and risk inadvertently pandering to the populist Unenlightenment of our own times. I'm thinking way back, too, to Tolstoy's dogmatic insistence that the only valid art was that which could be immediately apprehended by Russian peasants, so that meant for Tolstoy, Shakespeare was crap. George Orwell counter-denounced Tolstoy's attitude as aiming 'to narrow the range of human consciousness' – in today's parlance, dumbing-down, the patronising assumption that working folk aren't up to the more probing works of literature and the other arts. But I would put it to you that while Corrie's work might not be 'intellectual', it has keen intellect behind it, and while it may not be the most obvious carrion for academics to pick over, it illuminates no less than say, Zola or Lawrence, certain corners of experience that the literary world has on the whole been content to leave in the subterranean dark.

The Poetry of George Bruce

Growing up in Fraserburgh, on the tip of the north-east, and where the Moray Firth meets the North Sea, George Bruce knew the value of small communities, and also how they related to the wider world, both for good and ill. In his poem 'Kinnaird Head', Bruce wrote:

> This is the outermost edge of Buchan.
> Inland the sea birds range,
> The tree's leaf has salt upon it,
> The tree turns to the low stone wall.
> And here a promontory rises towards Norway.

Elsewhere, he refers to the local Greig family, of whom certain members emigrated to Norway, and of whom one became that country's most famous composer, Edvard Grieg, best known for his music for Henrik Ibsen's play *Peer Gynt*. For Bruce, the perspectives you could acquire by living and working on the coast were of infinite value. Further south along that coast, Fife inspired one of his most resonant poems, 'A Gateway to the Sea – At the East Port, St Andrews'. Of the ancient cathedral and university town, a small town, Bruce celebrated a significance which extended well beyond its boundaries, and homed in on its interactions with that wider world: 'The European sun knew those streets'. This poem moved me so much that I quoted it at the end of my book of short stories, *Slavonic Dances* (2017). At the conclusion of each of these three tales, a Scot who has had a relationship with Eastern Europe finds him or herself looking from a Fife shore in an easterly direction. Bruce's poem evokes the ruins of St Andrews Cathedral; here are its last lines:

> Under the touch the guardian stone remains
> Holding memory, reproving desire, securing hope
> In the stop of water, in the lull of night
> Before dawn kindles a new day.

Bruce's generation knew only too well that the future of Europe, and of their Scotland as part of Europe, couldn't be taken for granted. He himself passed his childhood in the shadow of World War One and lived through World War Two. In his writings, he displays a keen, if sombre, interest in the literatures of Europe. Writers such as Franz Kafka (1883-1924), a German-speaking Czech Jew from Prague, could evoke the sinister 'progress' of the twentieth century, in a Europe increasingly alienated and dehumanised. George Bruce knew the need for a spiritual wake-up call: 'In our mass produced society,' he wrote, 'where the beginnings and ends of things are rarely seen by one person, life does not present itself as a meaningful tale [...] The point at which [...] experience generalises itself is where particular places, domestic things, are seen and felt as belonging to an order of experience that we can all share, because it is part of human history.'

George Bruce's working life was marked by variety, and as such – together with the powerful influences of his Fraserburgh upbringing – he was able to draw on wide experience to match, and to enrich, his wide-ranging imagination. He taught at Dundee High School, commuting between there and Wormit on the Fife side of the Tay, and later became a BBC producer, responsible for programmes in literature, music and the visual arts (indeed, his keen interest in the other arts, Scottish and international, fed into his poetry – as witness, for example, his poems on the Polish pianist-composer Chopin and the Dutch painter Rembrandt). Having been a student at Aberdeen University, and eventually settling in Edinburgh, he had a relationship to all four of Scotland's major cities, as well as, of course, its smaller towns and communities.

I first met him in 1983, when I became involved in the teaching of an evening class in Scottish literature at St Andrews University. It was a ten-week course; I taught the first eight classes and George was responsible for the last two. The planning stage involved exchanges of letters between us and the Extra-Mural Department's head, and in due course George and I met in person. I will never forget how stimulated I was by his lectures and the passion with which he recalled a detail from his youth – the dumping of unsold herring in the sea at a time when malnourished children were suffering from rickets in the Glasgow slums: couldn't the fish have been quickly transported there? Injustice and inequality would rouse this warm-hearted man to sudden fury. His generous emotions as a man have always added a special poignancy to my reading of his poetry.

After I became the first librarian of the Scottish Poetry Library in 1984, I got to know George better as he was a frequent visitor. During the late 1980s and early 90s, we occupied two floors of the premises in Edinburgh's Tweeddale Court in the Old Town. The upstairs flat was used for visiting poets from overseas and also for the annual Library Christmas party. George always had a party piece (and more) for us and the atmosphere was electrifying.

The year 1999 marked both his 90th birthday and the launch of his book *Pursuit: Poems 1986-1998*; as ever, George was the life and soul. He was not a big man physically but the energy was closely packed within him, always ready to burst into expansive (and often quirkily comic) poetry. You were always aware of how his work resonated with a deep regard for Scotland and with the wider world of which it was a part.

It was said of him that, as he got older, his thoughts turned back to his youth in the north-east and to the Scots language – the Doric – to which, though it had never left him, he returned as a medium for his poetry. In 1991, the Mercat Press of Edinburgh published my anthology of contemporary poetry in Scots, *The New Makars*. At a launch party, George told me that when he received my invitation to contribute, he had said to himself, 'Fit am I going to send to Tom Hubbard?' He went on to tell me how: 'In the middle o the nicht, I woke up and lowped oot o the bed and stertit to write some lines o the poem I sent ye'. The poem was 'Weys o Self-Preservin Natur' and the north-east coastal theme is clear as the poet handles a clam-shell fossil:

Aince there stirred under this shall – life.
I thocht o the bearers o the chyne o life
that would gang on and on or lang deid this haund,
and yet the mair I vrocht at thocht
the mair I kent hoo peerie was the thocht.

In the summer of 2002, I was returning from a conference in the Netherlands and at Waverley Station I bumped into Duncan Glen, Scottish poet/publisher and a friend, who told me that George had died. In less than a year, early in 2003, Greta Thunberg was born. It was as if George was making way for the upcoming generations: I think he'd have issued his trademark chuckle at that. Many of his poems display a sense of ecological urgency such as has stirred Ms

Thunberg and her friends to action. Scotland's green movement –
and not only the movement – could well take heed of the writings
of George Bruce.

While re-reading George's autobiographical essays, I was much
taken by his story of how his father gave him a row when he caught
him walking dangerously on narrow planks at the harbour's edge. I
couldn't help but recall him telling us how, when well into his 80s
(and even 90s?) his daughter gave him a row for running to catch a
bus. I think that when we get older we become more aware of the
generations on either side of us – we say to our sons, daughters,
nephews and nieces, 'You take after your gran / grandad' – and so
we experience a strong desire both to honour the past and to hope
for the future.

In 1979, as he reached 70, his thoughts turned to those early
years in Fraserburgh and he extracted a wider meaning from the
area's two main occupations, farming and fishing: 'Whereas each
piece of landscape draws attention by its difference from any other
to locality, the sea proclaims its universality'. That observation
sums up much of the significance of his poetry. It informs his
poem 'Aberdeen, the Granite City':

The town secured by folk that warsled
With water, earth and stone; quarrying,
Shaping, smoothing their unforgiving stone […]

From the other side of the country, here's his 'Castle Tioram, Loch
Moidart':

The tide comes in and empties the castle
of all its bloody memories […]

The day's tourists have departed in time before the causeway
returns underwater; kids have been playing in a scene of once
terrible beauty, but now:

[…] Night,
skraichs – the sea birds have it for themselves.

Beyond Scotland, George's deep love and respect for mainland
European cultures is eloquently expressed in poems such

as 'Chopin at 10 Warriston Crescent – 1848', on the great Polish exile's recital at the house which would one day belong to one of George's Edinburgh neighbours; at the time of his tour of Scotland, Chopin was already near to his early death:

> It wis the cold that got ye
> and yon twisty stairs; you sclimmin
> them like yer hert tae burst. […]
> you soon't oot a' rooms and ha's
> and ower a' watters tae Europe
> and across the plains wi snaw […]

Set that beside George's splendid evocation of a small Danish town with its painted houses and cobbled streets, the birthplace of that country's best-known writer:

> …the fairy tale was written into the stones
> and waited for the poor boy to grow
> to tell the tales that knocked on doors
> at nights like drums that drummed, 'All's well!'

('At H C Andersen's Hus – Odense')

A fellow poet and contemporary of George Bruce's was Tom Scott (1918-95), who wrote of yet another Scottish poet that 'if Scotland were truly Scotland, his lines would be on everyone's lips'. Scott's words, I believe, apply equally to the poetry of George Bruce.

The Indian Summer of Lillias Scott Forbes

The vintage pamphlet was one in a batch donated to the Scottish Poetry Library. It intrigued me: its author was unknown to me, and when I asked around even those who had been familiar with her in the past weren't sure what had become of her. I had a sense that the mystery would remain. What I didn't know then was that her work had been warmly praised by no less a mandarin of Scottish poetry than Hugh MacDiarmid, and that she was still working away quietly in Fife; the real harvest was yet to come.

I first met her in Kirkcaldy in 1998, by which time she was a spirited near-octogenarian, and a contributor to Ian Nimmo White's new magazine *Fife Lines*. Friendship developed on both poetic and musical fronts: I learned that she was the daughter of the composer Francis George Scott (1880-1958) and the wife of another composer, Erik Chisholm (1904-65). F G Scott had been a mentor of Hugh MacDiarmid and had made song settings of Scottish poems; his son-in-law acted likewise, including his wife's poems (in Scots) in the corpus of his collaborations with writers.

Lillias's poetry possesses many qualities that we'd associate more with music: her 'Brown's Piece Barn' has the inevitability of a folk-song – 'Was it Katie I kissed or brown-eyed, low-browed Bess?' – and I found myself hearing something not unlike Patrick Kavanagh's 'On Raglan Road', and its speaker's fateful encounter with a dark-haired Dublin lass; as someone who is part-Irish, I could hear a lilt of Hibernian English in Lillias's poem:

Till the day 'twas ordained by flick of the master's finger
That the door be barred: the horses put out to new pasture
And our longed-for laughter would rise to the rafters no more
Oh, bring back the dancing, the stumbling, the tumbling,
 the fearful fumbling
At back of old Brown's Peace Barn as it was before!

Lillias and I discovered a common interest in French literature and culture. In her case, it goes back to childhood and regular visits to France, which in many ways was a musical spiritual home to her father. Some of the most moving pieces in her only book-length collection, *Views from the Bench: My Life in Poetry* (Grace

Note Publications, 2011) are evocations of the South, and of Paris around the Boul' St-Mich', as she reaches across time and space to that which had been lost. It's tougher, this, than mere nostalgia. You wouldn't catch her being sentimental about the Auld Alliance; true, she liked sitting in the 'French' cafés of St Andrews, but you got the sense that she was only too aware that it wasn't the real thing.

During her final years, and well into her 90s, she'd call me with the cry 'Give me work! I need work!' – by which she meant that she wanted me to keep on sending her selections of translatable francophone poetry from my (chaotic) library at home. I say 'francophone' because her interests ventured beyond the bounds of the Hexagon. She took quickly to the work of the nineteenth-century Swiss poet Alice de Chambrier, who died young but who had been praised by the ageing Victor Hugo. Her version of one of Alice's poems has something of the eldritch ballad-like quality that she knew so well from her roots in the Scottish Borders: here are the first two stanzas from her translation of 'C'était dans un vieux cimetière' as titled 'Butterie' (butterfly):

In darksome crannies o yon auld kirkyaird
Here lurk the yirdit hooses o the deid,
Shy-like, coorin doon neath the tangle o gerse
Frae the claw-haund o the moul, smoorin a thing aheid.

Frae oot the gloam there leams a gauntin stane
Abune the lave, storm-blasted, riven in twa –
An – croon o aa – doon flichtrin frae the hicht
A butterie, richt donsie in its faa.

(From *Lallans* magazine, Nummer 59, Hairst 2001)

Latterly, she was tackling Québec's *poète maudit* Emile Nelligan. She worked her way through other texts – I often chose for her poems about music – and her collected translations could well form her first posthumous volume, unless her memoirs, extant in typescript, get there first.

There's a reference in one of the poems reprinted in *View from the Bench*, to Sully-André Peyre's literary magazine *Marsyas,* which published work in both French and Provençal. During my last-ever research days for BOSLIT (the online Bibliography of Scottish Literature in Translation), I was in the Bibliothèque Nationale (BN), attempting to fulfil a promise I'd made to Lillias – to track down a French translation of one of her poems. It had been in *Marsyas*, sometime in the early 1950s, but she hadn't been sure of the exact date. I called up all the issues, went through them, and was about to give up when – there it was! The BN's holding was too fragile for a photocopy but we were able to obtain one from another library.

We've come a long way from the 1980s, when documentation of the poetry of Lillias Scott was hard to come by, and indeed when it seemed she'd been forgotten by the Scottish literati. The complete œuvre has still to appear. Almost of a sudden, though, she made her 'comeback' – she'd never been away! – in the late 1990s and beyond: it was an Indian summer for the poet whom we now know as Lillias Scott Forbes (1918-2013) after her second husband John Forbes, who had taught at Madras College in St Andrews.

Two further poetry pamphlets were published: Duncan Glen of Akros brought out *Turning a Fresh Eye* (1998), and from Colin Will of the Calder Wood Press there appeared *A Hesitant Opening of Parasols* (2009), the title reflecting her sense of the quirkiness of this life. She was appearing in anthologies and she recorded her poetry for the Scotstoun label (*Skreich o Day*, SSCD 134). A further CD, *Songs for a Year and a Day*, including a selection of her poems as set by Erik Chisholm, was recorded by Brad Liebl (baritone) at the University of Cape Town in 2000. This has been followed up (2021) by more Lillias-Erik settings on the disc *Chisholm: Songs* (Delphian DCD 34259), sung by Mhairi Lawson, Nicky Spence and Michael Mofidian, accompanied on the piano by Iain Burnside, and with booklet notes by the composer and poet John Purser.

In the summer of 2013, *View from the Bench* was due to be celebrated by Grace Note Publications at a reading and recital – introduced by Professor Margaret Bennett – at the Royal Conservatoire of Scotland. Lillias was too ill to attend. My wife and I visited her at a care home in St Andrews on the last Sunday in September that year, and she reminisced about her friends Edwin and Willa Muir who, among so much else, were the first translators of Franz Kafka into English and as working travellers knew both the light and the dark of European sensibility. On the following Wednesday morning, her nephew rang me to tell me that Lillias had made her last flitting overnight.

In the *Herald*'s obituary, Professor Alan Riach wrote of how Lillias's 'lyric grace and wicked sense of humour are there… reminding us how to chuckle and take pleasure in the everyday, see through all shams and pretentions, reach deep into memories, delight in subtle and flamboyant colours, to take on the difficult things, and always be open to love.'

Hamish Henderson as Translator

A knowledge of languages is an asset during a war: one of Hamish Henderson's duties, as a serving officer, was to interrogate captured Germans. His fluency in German and Italian links his army and artistic / scholarly careers. (The French have a special penchant for the military-literary complex: think of De Gaulle's memoirs, and his remark when called on to jail Jean-Paul Sartre – 'One does not put Voltaire in the Bastille'.)

Henderson's *Elegies for the Dead in Cyrenaica* (1948) are rightly considered to carry an echo of Rilke's *Duino Elegies*. (Alec Finlay recalls Henderson reciting Rilke's poetry in the bath.) Take these lines from the Scot's *Elegies*:

> Neither by dope of reportage, nor by an anodyne of statistics
> is *their* lot made easier: laughing couples at the tea-dance
> ignore their memory, the memoirs almost slight them
> and the queue forming up without thought to those dead,
> – O, to right them
> what requiem can I sing in the ears of the living?

This has the ring familiar from Rilke, as in these satirical lines on the shallowness of the twentieth century:

> How an Angel would trample it down beyond trace,
>   their market of comfort
> with the church alongside, bought ready for use: as clean
> and disenchanted and shut as the Post on a Sunday.
> (Translation: J B Leishman)

A 1981 article by Richard E Ziegfeld stresses the differences between Rilke and Henderson. These can be summed up – crudely, I admit – as Rilke's individualistic, uncannily mystical invocations, and as contrasted with Henderson's social and political concerns grounded in an undogmatic dialectical materialism. Rilke strove to give 'things', the transitory entities of this life, a permanence guaranteed by the impalpable permanence ('immortality' to put it unsubtly) of art. 'We are the bees of the invisible', wrote Rilke of the poet's role. 'Tremulously we gather in the honey of the Visible to store up the great golden hive of the Invisible.' Henderson could be said to do the opposite: he turns abstract notions into concrete images. (In effect, Rilke does that too).

The best-known and most large-scale of Henderson's translation projects are his version of the *Prison Letters* of Antonio Gramsci. This was first published during the 1970s in several issues of the *New Edinburgh Review*, and reappeared in book form in 1988. For men of the left like Henderson, post-1956 and that year's revelations of Stalinist brutality, Gramsci offered an alternative model: far from the orthodox (and secularly Calvinistic) notion of 'existence' determining 'consciousness', Gramsci in effect reversed that formula: consciousness could indeed impact on existence, the subject on the object, or to put it less abstrusely, cultural phenomena could influence economic-political-social reality. Gramsci's thought restored a creative dialectic to the Marxian tradition after decades of grey stasis. (A younger Scottish thinker, Tom Nairn, also came under the influence of Gramsci.)

The key word was hegemony: the heirs of Gramsci went on to argue that a complex of establishment iconography, advertising and top-down entertainment could – often subliminally – causes people to make political choices at odds with their objective economic interests. More recently we have witnessed the results in Trump, Brexit, and their attendant chaos.

Henderson found a corrective in a culture created *by* the people rather than *for* the people, and in Scotland pioneered the collection and revival of folk tradition, which in turn influenced original creative work. In Scotland, the corpus of folk art and that of 'high' art are not always in contention, despite the efforts of Henderson's friend, fellow-poet and sparring partner, Hugh MacDiarmid, to assert otherwise.

Henderson's translations of German, Italian and Greek poetry, curiously, are not so well known. The poets include his beloved Hölderlin; Eugenio Montale; Dino Campana; C P Cavafy. As regards that last-named, Henderson – like many north Europeans before him (eg. Goethe, Ibsen) – responded to the vitality and sensuality of the south:

Passer-by,
If you are from Alexandria, you will not blame me.
You know the fury, the pace of our life here: –

What ardour there is, what extreme pleasure.
  (Cavafy, 'Tomb of Iasis')

The Germans had their own distinct and typically philosophical take on Greek culture, not least Hölderlin: Henderson's version of his 'Socrates and Alcibiades' concludes:

He who has thought the most loves the fullness of life;
Highest virtue is prized by him who has looked on the world:
  And often the wisest turn
  To beauty in the end of all.

Scandic Scots:
Some Scots–Scandinavian Poetic Connections

In Strindberg's novel *Röda Rummet* (*The Red Room*)[1], which was published in 1879, one of the characters makes an extremely provocative speech at a public meeting. Olle Montanus maintains that Sweden does not really exist because so many people from neighbouring countries have settled there.

> During the reign of Gustavus Adolphus a whole cargo of Scottish vermin landed, joined the army and wormed their way into the aristocracy. On the East coast there are many families still holding to the traditions they brought with them when they immigrated from Livonia and other Slavonic provinces, which is why we so often come across pure Tartar types in this country... In my opinion the Swedish nation is doing its best to become denationalized. Open the Swedish Book of Heraldry and count the Swedish names you find. If there are more than 25 per cent of them, gentlemen, you may cut off my nose!

This causes such an uproar in the hall that he barely escapes with his features intact.

Of course the reality is that Scottish-Scandinavian influences have been two-way. There's a great deal more to this than the familiar blood-and-guts, whether Viking raids or Scottish mercenaries. I want to concentrate on the Scots language and its poetry, and how they have been enriched by their sister-cultures at the other side of the North Sea. Perhaps some day the two-way principle could extend to Scots-language poetry finding an audience in the Scandinavian countries. There may be scope for creative dialogue with such cultures as Sami, Faroese and Greenlandic, as well as with the 'mainstream'.

Scots is a north European language in its own right. We have at least two other languages in Scotland: English, obviously the dominant and the most official; Gaelic, a Celtic tongue related to Irish and now spoken mainly in the Highlands. Gaelic does have some semi-official recognition. Scots has no such status whatever, although it was once the official language of our country. It still suffers from the misconception that it is merely a vulgar dialect of English. Unlike Gaelic, Scots is not taken seriously as a language by the Government – or with honourable exceptions – by those in the media. Gaelic is now fashionable: ready for taming?

Scots is capable of aristocratic elegance, and of a continental sophistication, somewhat owing to the French influence; yet it also has an earthy, lower-class directness of expression. This all seems to be too much for the effete parochialism of Scotland's kulturniks.

In *The Scotsman* of 5th January 1991, two news items appeared on the same page. A sizeable headline announced a Government cash boost of £1.5 million for Gaelic television, enabling the TV companies to treble the hours of broadcasting in Gaelic. Tucked away in a corner was a snippet on an appeal to raise £50,000 for a Scots Language Resource Centre. No Scots activist worth the name will grudge a penny that goes towards Gaelic, especially if the Gaels use some of the money to demonstrate solidarity with Scots – as well as with other suppressed language cultures overseas.

Literary events during Glasgow's European city of culture year (1990) consistently marginalised Scots to the point of virtual exclusion. We need not count token gestures. This fate, happily, was not shared by Gaelic, but it did mean that overseas visitors were deprived of an essential part of our home-grown European culture.

Regarding the future, I could describe my outlook as existential, paradoxical. In other words I have hope but not optimism. I have become too wary of optimism, that opium of the Scottish intelligentsia.

I work at the Scottish Poetry Library, where I am the Librarian. Over the years this Library has fostered literary contacts between Scotland and other north European countries; to this end we have cooperated with the Danish Cultural Institute, the Scottish-Finnish Society and now Edinburgh University's Department of Scandinavian Studies. It was a heartening experience when the Library received a party of school pupils from northern Jutland, from Thisted – birthplace of the great Danish writer Jens Peter Jacobsen. As the students were arriving at the Library, a leading Scottish composer, Ronald Stevenson, was leaving. In the courtyard he treated them to a spontaneous mini-seminar on the music of Carl Nielsen.

I had prepared a small chart to show our guests just how much

Scots was closer to Danish than it was to English:

DANISH	SCOTS	ENGLISH
barn	bairn	child
bygge	bigg	build
edderkop	ettercap	spider
flytte	flit	move (home)
fremmed	fremmit	strange, foreign
græde	greet	cry, weep
hjerne	harn	brain
kende	ken	know
mørk	mirk	dark
skrive	scrieve	write
tom	tume	empty

These are just a few of many examples. Then we played a tape of Scottish poetry, much of it in Scots. I think I said to the students: 'Don't worry if you don't understand most of it, just enjoy the sound.' In fact the students told me that they could follow the Scots reasonably well. One of them even jotted a list of Scots words that she could recognise from their Danish versions.[2]

Three years ago [in 1987] I took part in a European poetry festival in Belgium. At dinner a group of us were talking about our respective ballad traditions. There were a Dutchman, a Norwegian, a Hungarian, an Irishman, and me. It was fascinating for us to tell each other the ballad stories – I'd relate a Scottish one, and the Hungarian or the Dutchman would say, 'oh, we have a version of that!'.

Postmodernists would say that the ballads are out of date – we shouldn't take them as a model. Myself, I agree with the architect Berthold Lubetkin that postmodernism is the mumbo-jumbo of a hit-and-miss society. I also agree with Willa Muir when she relates how the Scottish ballads draw on the 'underworld of feeling'.[3] Garcia Lorca recognised the deep, suggestive, subconscious power of balladry when he based his own poetry on the folk idiom of Andalusia; this power he called the *duende* – which 'surges up from the soles of the feet… This is, in fact, the spirit of the earth.'[4]

Alexander Gray (1882-1968) was Professor of Economics at Edinburgh University and was also a skilled linguist and Scots-writing poet. He took many ballads and folk songs from Germany,

Switzerland, the Netherlands and Denmark and recast them in the Scots tongue, using the idiom of the Scottish ballads. He was particularly drawn to the Danish ballads and instinctively felt the affinity between the Danish and Scottish ballad cultures.[5]

Here are the introductory stanzas of a 'tale of enchantment' 'The Maid as Hind and Hawk' ('Jomfru i Fugleham' in the Danish original):

O, weel I ken whaur stands the forest:
It stands by the dark loch-side.
And bonnier trees you'll see there growin'
Than in a' the warld sae wide.

Ay, there the bonniest trees are growin'.
The saugh and the linden tree,
And there the noble beas' of the forest,
The hart and the doe rin free.

The hart and the doe and the rae rin free,
And a' the forest beasts;
And there in the wood rins the bonnie wee hind,
That bears the gowd under her breists.[5]

rae: roe, *gowd*: gold

Gray was at pains to justify his treatment of the Danish ballads. He declared that his aim was 'to tell the tale as a Scots balladist would have told the tale, had he decided to add it to his repertory.'[6] I do not myself believe that one can translate poetry. 'Translation' is not the word if one is making a new poem, in one's own culture, out of a poem in another culture. Like a piece of music, a poem is a construct of sound, and cannot exist in any form other than itself. I prefer the word *transcreation*, which I think relates to *transcription* in music. When Liszt transcribes Mozart's *Don Giovanni* for two pianos, he sheds an interesting light, from the outside, on Mozart's opera. When Scottish poets *transcreate* Scandinavian poetry into Scots or English they are not pretending to reproduce all the subtleties of the original – how can they? What they *are* doing is shining the light of their culture on to another. Put in another way, 'translation' of poetry implies that you're trying to produce an identical twin of the original, if in different clothes. With transcreation the relationship is not that of identical twins, but perhaps more of brother and sister – that is, the original poem and the new poem are closely related, but different. Like brother and sister, there's a bond between them, but also a certain tension.

Let us turn from standard Scots to a form of the language spoken in the Shetland islands. Orkney and Shetland were originally ruled by Norway before they were transferred to Scotland in the late fifteenth century. Over the years Norn, the Scandinavian tongue of Shetland, became so admixed with Scots words that now the Scots is predominant. However, the Norse influence is still strong, and several poets today are writing in Shetlandic Scots. My new all-Scots anthology, *The New Makars*, includes the work of William Tait, Rhoda Bulter and a poet not long into his thirties, Robert Alan Jamieson. Shetlandic is natural to them all. One of the anthology's Shetlandic poems is William Tait's 'Furnenst da Day'. It consists of six stanzas; the last is a recapitulation of the first. Here are the opening two:

Furnenst da day
I hain my sairest loss
An caa my nain
Da heft I canna hae.

Da gold I yird
Oonseen dis simmer nycht
'S a solya's sheen
On hairsts A'll never hird.[7]

furnenst: against, *da:* the; *hain:* save; *caa:* call;
my nain: my own, *heft:* precious possession; *hae:* have;
yird: bury: *simmer nycht:* summer night; *solya:* brief
burst of sunshine; *hairsts:* harvests, *hird:* garner.

The Shetlanders have a word *bonhoga* which roughly means 'the place of one's childhood', 'roots… the source of all our being'. This is not totally unrelated to Garcia Lorca's *duende*. William Tait, who is in his early seventies, returned to Shetland after a long absence and now lives in the house where he was born

George Campbell Hay (1915 84) was a linguistic phenomenon.

He was an extremely rare kind of Scottish poet – one who wrote in all three of our languages, Gaelic, Scots and English. He had a command of many other tongues. He wrote an original poem in Norwegian, and transcreated the Danish poet L C Nielsen into Scots. Nielsen's 'Digt fra Dover' must have struck a chord in Hay, who came from the Argyll fishing village of Tarbert:

> They cerried a drooned sailor bye;
> the music struck up solemnly.
>
> The kist was as nerra as a bunk aa;
> lourd it hung frae their haunds ablow.
>
> ...
>
> Slaw, slaw an' stieve they paced.
> Him that's deid has nae haste.[8]

cerried: carried, *drooned*: drowned, *kist*: coffin, *nerra*: narrow, *lourd*: heavy, *ablow*: below, *slaw*: slow, *stieve*: steady, *deid*: dead

George Campbell Hay was neglected in his lifetime and we have yet to come to terms with the full range of his work. He was also a composer.

Fortunately, the artist Archie MacAlister has done much to promote Hay's work by means of exhibitions and publications and the young Gaelic scholar, Michel Byrne, is preparing a collected edition.

Robin Fulton was for many years editor of the Scottish literary magazine *Lines Review*. During his tenure he cultivated connections with Swedish, Danish and Norwegian poets and since then has established himself as one of the leading transcreators, into English, of contemporary Scandinavian poetry. In *Four Swedish Poets* (Fredonia: White Pine Press, 1990), Fulton gives us versions of work by Lennart Sjögren, Eva Ström, Kjell Espmark and Tomas Tranströmer. Fulton now teaches in Stavanger. He does not himself compose in Scots, but he was a friend and collaborator of Robert Garioch (1909-81). Garioch, or Geerie as he was known, was the quintessential makar. 'Makar' is that Scots word for 'poet' which emphasises the craftsman, the maker. Garioch was one of our most skilled.craftsmen in verse. In *Lines Review*, no. 36, Fulton made English versions of Swedish poems, and Garioch turned them into standard Scots. In Tranströmer's poem 'Lisbon' we have a northerner's treatment of a very southern subject: the Alfama, the old quarter of the Portuguese capital, with its labyrinth of narrow lanes. Here there are two prisons. One is for thieves, who wave through the barred windows, shouting for their photographs to be taken.

'Bit bere,' said the guide, snicheran like to split his-sel
'here sit politicians.' I saw the facade the facade the facade
and heich up in a windae a man
that stude wi a keekan-gless til his ee and luikit
outowre the sea.[9]

snicheran: giggling, *his-sel:* himself, *heich:* high, *windae:* window, *stude:* stood, *keekan-gless:* telescope, *ee:* eye, *luikit:* looked

On that enigmatic note, we conclude our own attempt to look across either side of that sea which separates Scotland and Scandinavia.

NOTES:

1 August Strindberg, *The Red Room: Scenes of Artistic and Literary Life*, translated by Elizabeth Sprigge (London: Everyman's Library, 1967), p. 222.

2 For an authoritative account of Scots-Scandinavian linguistic connections, see David Murison, 'Norse Influence on Scots', *Lallans* No. 13 (Mairtinmas 1979), pp 31-34.

3 Willa Muir, *Living with Ballads* (London: The Hogarth Press, 1965), p. 53.

4 *Lorca*, introduced and selected by J L Gili (Harmondsworth: Penguin Books, 1960), p. 127.

5 Alexander Gray, *Four and Forty: a selection of Danish ballads presented in Scots* (Edinburgh: The University Press, 1954), pp 93-4.

6 ibid., p. xiv.

7 *The New Makars: The Mercat anthology of contemporary poetry in Scots*, edited by Tom Hubbard (Edinburgh: James Thin, The Mercat Press, 1991). Mr Tait reads 'Furnenst da Day', and a selection of his other

poems, on the cassette *Twa Chiels and a Lass* (Glasgow: Scotsoun, 1979). [NOTE: This recording is now available on CD].

8 George Campbell Hay, 'Digt fra Dover – Poem frae Dover frae the Danish of L C Nielsen', *Scottish International* (February 1972), p. 33.

9 *Lines Review* No.36 (March 1971), p. 19.

Scotland and Poland

In the autumn of 1990, at the end of a guest lecture at the University of Mainz, I noticed a familiar face in my audience. I couldn't quite place him, but he re-introduced himself as Tomasz Kitlinski. Of course – he was the bright theatre worker I'd met in Lublin, Poland, a year and a half before. I'd been on a Ricky Demarco-led 'expedition' and we'd mingled with visual and performing artists in the south-eastern Polish city which had once been a thriving centre of Jewish culture.

My hosts in Mainz invited Tomasz to join our dinner party that evening. He was in Germany for a year's study of the philosophy of Schelling, and as we walked together on that crisp night to our respective digs, he revealed a well-informed admiration for the work of Alasdair Gray. I was astonished: how, at that time, had he become so familiar with the Scottish author? Could I have named one contemporary Polish writer, let alone been able to discuss their work? Need I add that Tomasz was more knowledgeable about Alasdair Gray than I was...

Twenty years on, and based on a 2009 conference, *Scotland and Poland* is to be welcomed by all who wish greater understanding between our two countries. Mutual incomprehension has, over the centuries, been beset by hostility at worst and sentimentality at not so best. A leitmotif of the book is that Scottish ignorance of Poland has far exceeded Polish ignorance of Scotland. An expecially inglorious example, several times invoked in the book, was the wartime Scottish working-class left's knee-jerk objection to the anti-Sovietism of Polish soldiers stationed here; this was matched by native Protestant shoutiness against the mainly RC incomers. In many cases, writes Peter D Stachura, both these unwelcoming parties came together in 'an incongruous *mélange* of the Red and the Orange'.

Earlier stishies between Lion and Eagle possessed a more comic character, and again much invoked are the not very nice things said by Scottish Latin-writing poet John Barclay (1582-1621) about the Poles; his contemporary, the politician and political philosopher Łukasz Opaliński, was only too happy to reply in kind. William Lithgow, another Scottish contemporary wandering-Scot (and hands-wandering chancer), called Poland's then-capital, Kraków, a town 'of small importance', but he was in the habit of slagging off various continental peoples, and took a particular scunner at the Hungarians.

Generally, though, the Scots and the Poles have worked out ways to get on well with each other: wise policy, because in many ways they have become each other. The earlier diasporas were of Scots to Poland, and Peter P Bajer is right to champion 'the underrated role' of Scottish women in the welfare of their communities and in the maintenance of identity. Identity, that is, subject to metamorphosis. There's a fine poem by Dundonian makar Matthew Fitt which, though it's not mentioned in this book, does adumbrate much of what is expanded here: 'intil poland's hert an centuries' blood / tae kythe as surgeons, teachers, brewsters o beer / reckoners o five year plans – Czamer [Chalmers], Czochranek [Cochranes], Kabrun [Cockburns], Makalienski [MacLeans], Wajer [Weirs]' ('Schotten'). Living in Kirkcaldy, I'm daily aware of the book's focus on the coastal defences constructed by Polish soldiers: the dog and I can clamber about the great grey blocks along the beach. I grew up alongside kids who had Polish dads and Scottish mums, and yes, hereabouts we well know the tales of wartime romances: all that hand-kissing, the smart uniforms, the jealous indigenous menfolk. Until well into the 1980s you could hear Polish spoken by elderly people in Kirkcaldy High Street, then it fell silent, to be resumed by the generation arriving here in the wake of Poland's 2004 membership of the EU. Our current Polish deli is only a few doors along from a much earlier incarnation, Kalisz's. I have a distant family connection in that my great-grandparents acquired a Polish grandson-in-law; I used to speculate that a shared Catholic background may have eased that process, a phenomenon to which the book makes frequent reference, but I learned that my family had increasingly distanced itself from the old faith.

Scotland and Poland offers a judicious variety of personal anecdote and academic rigour. Most of the contributors are professional historians, and often economic historians at that. Those of us who are not of that calling may find the tables and statistics on the dry side, but they are absolutely necessary for a factual foundation of comparative study in all fields including the arts (of which more later). Robert L Frost notes that modernisation, in Poland, has been viewed as preferable to backward feudalism, whereas in Scotland the new order was condemned for destroying the values of the clan. Professor Frost suggests that we ought rather 'to reappraise the black and white legends, and to escape the long intellectual shadow cast by the Enlightenment, to look anew at the rural economies of Poland-Lithuania and the Highlands from below, not above, with peasants as economic actors, rather than passive victims of oppression or romanticised figures in a mythical, timeless world.' We might argue with that, and it's as well to have the terms of contention thus set out.

A notable slippage of academic objectivity occurs when Professor Stachura cites the 1928 programme of the National Democratic Party, which proclaimed that the Polish state 'must' be based on the principles of Roman Catholicism. He continues: 'Progressive' ideas regarding divorce, abortion and sexual licence attracted minimal popular sympathy because these were perceived as pernicious and 'un-Polish'. In short, the Second Republic had a definite, admirable moral compass.' One doesn't have to be a Protestant or atheist bigot (nor indeed a committed libertine) to find this more than a little unnerving. However, it does shed inadvertent light on the vexed relationship, in present-day Poland, between Catholic nationalism and free-market capitalism. On a research visit in 2002, I noticed that the street renamed after John Paul II was infested with sex shops, and one of the walls of the Royal Palace (rebuilt from plans, post-war) was draped with a massive Coca-Cola ad.

As the book progresses, social and economic history becomes also increasingly cultural. The concept of 'New Scots', drawn from the recent Polish diaspora, poses questions of the nature of nationalism, Polish and Scottish, and how this is predicated on ethnic or civic criteria. The first and last chapters present us with clues as to how to take all this forward. The book concludes with a charmingly informal piece by a non-academic, an Edinburgh-based art consultant called Grażyna Fremi: she has been involved in sterling efforts to make Polish culture better appreciated within Scotland. She offers us an invaluable documentation of the various bodies who are active in this field. The opening chapter is Neal Ascherson's address to the 2009 conference: it's a wealth of scene-setting details, such as a reference to the charismatic Scottish soldier who features in Henryk Sienkiewicz's historical novel *Pan Wołodyjowski* (1888), and a salute to Richard Demarco's eminently consequential attraction – as a European-minded, Italo-Scottish, post-war teenager – to the matter of Poland.

Thus framed, the book seems to me to call out for another book to follow it up, and Neal Ascherson is the person best placed to write it. *Scotland and Poland* also suggests to me that its range of scholars needs to be matched by a team working in cultural fields, now that the present book has so meticulously (and eloquently) achieved the socio-economic groundwork. In music, Chopin's visit to Scotland is well-known, not so much composer Erik Chisholm's invitation to Karol Szymanowski to perform in Glasgow. Ronald Stevenson has enjoyed an intimate relationship with Polish music, notably that of Paderewski, whose opera *Manru* is the basis for a piano suite, both sprightly and lyrical, by the Scottish composer. Stevenson is also the author of a short monograph on Paderewski. In the visual arts, in addition to the efforts of Demarco and his co-workers, Jeremy Howard is a St Andrews historian of *art nouveau*, equally illuminating on its Scottish and Polish manifestations. If only Scottish literary academia could be roused from its comfort zones and work along similar lines (comparative lit, though it has had its doughty champions here, has not on the whole flourished in relation to Scottish lit). For example, we might then have studies which brought together literary and economic history, exploring representations of capitalist development in novels such as Władysław Reymont's *Ziemia obiecana* / *The Promised Land* (1899; filmed by Andrzej Wajda) and John MacDougall Hay's *Gillespie* (1914; filmed by nobody), the former in a more urban context (Łódź) than the latter. Moreover, just as *Scotland and Poland* reminds us of both countries' other 'auld alliances' – with France – another triangular relationship could yield much on the literary front: so, let's place together the American travelogues of contemporaries Robert Louis Stevenson and Henryk Sienkiewicz.

Much in *Scotland and Poland* suggested to me that in Scotland we have as rich a history and a culture as does Poland, but we tend to sit on it. Take music again: in recent years, the Poles have been reviving their native operatic repertoire, including the aforementioned *Manru*. Whatever happened to Robin Orr's RLS-based opera *Hermiston*, which wowed audiences back in the 1970s?

Of Scotland's (relative) lack of self-confidence, nothing in this book hinted more than the statement on the verso of the title-page: 'First Published in Great Britain'.

Erik Chisholm: a Scot among the Czechs

There are many beautiful Scottish songs which we rarely hear, if ever. Some were the work of Erik Chisholm, who was born in the Southside of Glasgow on 4th January 1904 and who died aged 61 on 8th June 1965. His death occurred in Cape Town, South Africa, where he had been professor of music at the city's university. The job was a great success for him professionally, but it was troublesome for him politically; he was working in South Africa during the apartheid régime and, as a man of the left, he received unwelcome attention from the state authorities.

There is a certain poignancy in the fact that his life ended so far from Europe, as he was an artist who was close to the continent's innovations in music during the twentieth century. Coming from a Scotland which had been thoroughly provincialised during the previous century, he was a key figure in the struggle to re-Europeanise, culturally, his native Scotland. In 1930, Chisholm was the driving force behind the new Active Society for the Propagation of Contemporary Music, which invited mainland European composers of the avant-garde to visit Scotland where their work would be performed. Among their number were the Hungarian Béla Bartók and the Pole Karol Szymanowski. Like these two, Chisholm in his own music went back to his country's ancient musical traditions and reconfigured them for a modern cosmopolitan world: this was very much an open-minded cultural nationalism at ease in its internationalism.

The 1930s were a testing time for cultural activists like Erik Chisholm, intent as they were on challenging the prevailing aesthetic conservatism of the backwater which Scotland was at that time. True, the so-called Scottish Renaissance, propelled by such literary figures as the poet Hugh MacDiarmid and his peers, was well underway, but again progress was not without its hitches, to put it mildly. Take the visual arts during this decade: the Society of Scottish Artists was in many ways the equivalent of Chisholm's Active Society for the Propagation of Contemporary Music, but its path of true love for the European avant-garde did not run smoothly.

In 1931, the Society of Scottish Artists organised the first exhibition in Britain, let alone Scotland, of work by the Norwegian

Edvard Munch. It was in genteel, repressed Edinburgh that the public were exposed to a European artist whose images were intensely erotic in content and intensely expressionistic in form. A letter to an Edinburgh newspaper complained that we should just stick with our comforting home-grown Scottish artists rather 'than bring any more of Munch's type to Edinburgh to vitiate the tastes of our youth'.

I suspect that if the Czech composer Leoš Janáček had been alive and able to travel, he'd have been invited to Scotland by Chisholm and his colleagues in the Active Society. But Janáček had died in 1928. Nevertheless, Erik Chisholm went on to write a highly readable and idiosyncratic monograph on Janáček's operas; sadly, Chisholm died before he could revise it, however it was edited by Ken Wright and posthumously published in 1971.

John Purser's critical biography of 2006, *Erik Chisholm: Scottish Modernist 1904-65: Chasing a Restless Muse*, is a book which should be in every Scottish library. Purser is not only one of Scotland's finest musicologists, he is himself a notable composer and also a poet. He is therefore very well placed to comment on the often literary nature of Chisholm's book on Janáček. Chisholm delighted in language as well as in music – and this is most appropriate for his subject, whose music is based on the speech cadences of Moravian Czech – not, as Purser points out, that Chisholm possessed any significant command of Czech. He didn't.

Erik Chisholm's book is a very writerly production, that's to say it's a book composed by someone who loves to communicate by means of an imaginative use of English, and it's no wonder that he was impelled to make song-settings of Scottish poetry. Purser argues that Chisholm's book does not always conform to the objective, technical nature of musical analysis: as an example of this, he cites Chisholm's commentary on the opening bars of *Jenůfa*, where the Scot writes of 'the dry crackling, cricket-like timbre [...] somehow the resulting effect is sinister, even threatening [...]'. Purser commends such writing for its vividness, but he also remarks that Chisholm backs up his 'writerly' remarks with due technical knowledge.

Erik Chisholm is strongly responsive to the literary works on which Janáček based his operas, and he writes illuminatingly on how these sources, novels and plays, are transmuted into a different artistic form. There is evidence in the book of Chisholm's knowledge of Russian literature, and this enriches his discussion of *From the House of the Dead*, which Janáček had based on Dostoyevsky's autobiographical novel on incarceration in Siberia, and also *Kát'a Kabanová*, which owes its existence to Aleksander Ostrovsky's play *The Storm*.

Chisholm as literary critic is aware that the leading protagonist of a novel, however much he may have in common with the author himself, is still an artistic construct and must not be confused with his creator. Chisholm refers to 'the fictitious build-up Dostoyevsky gives his hero, so it would be as well to accept the character as given by the novelist, rather than try – as some surely misguided producers of the opera have done – to make Petrovič [the novel's main character] look like Dostoyevsky'.

In his chapter on *Kát'a Kabanová*, Chisholm has regard to the literary sociology of nineteenth-century Russia: 'The novels of Tolstoy and Turgenev dealt mainly with the lives of the nobility and the peasants: it was left to Ostrovsky to reveal the shortcomings and the strong points of the merchant class'. (By way of a comic footnote, let me add that when Tchaikovsky met Andrew Carnegie in New York, he noted that the Scottish industrialist bore a distinct facial resemblance to Ostrovsky.)

Chisholm's chapter on Janáček's opera, *The Excursions of Mr Brouček*, is the longest chapter in the book. That's because it's dealing with an opera in two parts, as based on a sequence of two novels, and each part could be considered an opera in itself. Part One is *Mr Brouček's Excursion to the Moon*; Part Two is *Mr Brouček's Excursion to the Fifteenth Century*. Brouček's name means 'beetle' in Czech, and he is the archetypal petty-bourgeois philistine, complacent, vulgar, crass, devoted only to his bodily needs, chiefly of beer. He has no interest in the arts or in any kind of cultural idealism.

In the first part, Mr Brouček lurches out of the pub – the Vikárka, just opposite St Vitus Cathedral in Prague – and finds himself on a proto-surrealist journey to the moon, where he encounters characters who are his complete opposite – ultra-refined aesthetes, and including a young lady with the name of Etherea.

Chisholm discusses Janáček's literary source, the 1880s novel-series, *The Excursion of Mr Brouček*, by the poet and satirist Svatopluk Čech; he argues that though both Čech and Janáček intend to mock Mr Brouček for his philistinism, his opposites – the lunar aesthetes – are not really the ideal antidote to him: they are too ethereal, quite literally not down-to-earth enough (well, they are lunar), far too absorbed in their precious sensibilities. So the satire misses the point, and in contrast to these over-sophisticated beings who would hardly deign to get their hands dirty, Mr Brouček can actually come across as a more sympathetic fellow than we'd have expected: he has common sense, he is ordinary, unpretentious Joe Public with his only-too-human failings, what the French would call *l'homme moyen sensuel*, the average sensual man.

As ever, Chisholm pays careful attention to an opera's literary promptings, and indeed makes a striking comparison with another work of both literary and operatic significance – W S Gilbert's *Patience*, the basis for the comic opera with music by Arthur Sullivan. Chisholm notes that Čech's novel and Gilbert's drama appeared within a few years of each other in the 1880s. *Patience* was first performed in 1881 as an opera, but Gilbert's text has maintained its status in its own right as poetry: it's proved eminently quotable, as in those lines which sharply criticise the effete aesthete Bunthorne as he 'walk[s] down Piccadilly with a poppy or a lily in [his] medieval hand', his unhealthy complexion described as 'greenery-yallery' – greenish-yellow – which is the colour of that favourite strong drink – absinthe – of the *fin-de-siècle* decadents who were the successors of the most over-the-top aficionados of the Aesthetic Movement.

Chisholm points out that unlike Svatopluk Čech and Janáček, Gilbert was not at all intending to satirise the philistines: he was basically on their side, rather, when he mocked the aesthetes; after all, he was writing for a solid Victorian bourgeoisie who wanted lowbrow entertainment at the expense of the highbrows. Čech's and Janáček's anti-philistine intentions have somewhat backfired, and the supposed superiority of the aesthetes is undermined.

Erik Chisholm hasn't been the only Scot to write at length about Mr Brouček and his shenanigans. Jessie Scott was born in Edinburgh in 1914, married a Czech airman, and settled in Brno and its university as Professor Jessie Kocmanová. Her article on Čech's *Brouček* appeared in the journal *Brno Studies in English* and it is she who has introduced the second *Brouček* novel to speakers of English. She demonstrates that the anti-philistine thrust of the second book is stronger than it is in the first, as we have our Mr Brouček time-travelling to the fifteenth century and the era of the Hussites with their self-sacrificing, idealistic commitment to the

Czech nation.

Jessie Kocmanová notes Mr Brouček's hostility to the struggle for Czech culture, language and literature – he prefers the German language of the ruling powers. As a bachelor, he doesn't see why he should pay taxes for other people's kids to be educated in the indigenous culture – he'd rather spend his money on booze. We have no shortage of Mr Broučeks in Scotland.

Kocmanová wrote on the Scots language in another article in *Brno Studies in English*. Her regard for both Czech and Scots was shared by her fellow-Scot Erik Chisholm – one difference is that Kocmanová became fluent in Czech. In the course of his chapter on Janáček's *The Cunning Little Vixen*, Chisholm tells us that the libretto is written in a Brno dialect called Líšeň, and that this can baffle Prague singers and audiences, 'in much the same way', he continues, 'as the poems of Robert Burns in the Ayrshire dialect are puzzling to many English readers. In both cases there is a picturesque attraction, once the characteristic cadences of the language are appreciated'.

A strong leitmotif in Chisholm's book on Janáček is his reference to the composer's debt to Moravian folk music. Chisholm does not ignore those early operas which Janáček composed before he found his unique style. Indeed, the Scot is full of praise for the rarely-heard opera *Počatek romanu / The Beginning of a Romance*, which Janáček wrote in 1891. Chisholm detects the influence of Dvořák on this opera, and we should note here that Erik Chisholm was a recipient of the Dvořák Medal. He challenges those who have dismissed the work, and records his enjoyment of 'this bright little opera' when it was performed at the 1958 Brno Janáček Music Festival.

Chisholm even questions Janáček's own reservations about *The Beginning of a Romance*: 'Janáček later expressed regret at having introduced a number of folk-songs into his score, but to a foreign audience this is probably an attraction rather than otherwise'. Such a Scottish appreciation of Czech folk idiom in a sense reciprocates the interest of Czech cultural activists, during the nineteenth century and after, in the Scottish ballads. Naděžda Skřivánková's Charles University dissertation on the Scottish ballads emphasises their influence on their Czech counterparts.

Some of the loveliest of Erik Chisholm's own compositions are the song-settings he made of poems by his second wife, Lillias

Scott (1918-2013). She was the daughter of the composer Francis George Scott, mentor of Hugh MacDiarmid. Lillias came from the Scottish Borders country, the home of many of the classic Scottish ballads. Those of her own poems set by Erik Chisholm are mostly short lyrics, but one of them – recorded on the CD *Songs for a Year and a Day* – is the more ballad-like *The White Blood of Innocence*. This poem's theme of a man's seductive power over a young girl might recall the betrayals suffered by the heroines of *Jenůfa* and *Kát'a Kabanová*; it should not surprise us that the Scottish ballad, *The Demon Lover*, has been translated into Czech. However, Lillias's poem concludes in a tender manner of which the girl's ex-lover seems undeserving:

But tho' in lust ye saired me ill
My filit blude shone whiter still
In baith oor een reflectit fair –
For a' oor innocence wis there!

Doing Something Uncustomary:
Edwin Morgan and Attila József

Early in 2006, if you walked up Rákoczi Street, one of the main boulevards in the centre of Budapest, you would have seen a series of three posters. Each carried a different familiar image of the city together with a question in English.

The posters were in green, red and blue. The green one asked: 'Did you travel here to get to know the people or to be where people don't know you?' The red one asked: 'Did you travel here to get to know the culture or to get a break from your own?' The blue one asked: 'Did you travel here to get to know the customs or to do something uncustomary?' Most of us, I guess, would be willing enough to answer the red and blue questions, and be piously positive about the first part of the green one while hoping that no-one was going to probe us about its second part. I don't know how Edwin Morgan would answer either part of the green poster, but red and blue could help us obtain a perspective on his relationship with Hungarian poetry and, in particular, the work of Attila József.

There is a reasonable consensus that Morgan is Scotland's leading translator of poetry. His prolific output (Morgan, 1996) includes versions of poetry from French, German, Spanish, Italian, Russian and Hungarian cultures. Regarding the last, in addition to József he has addressed himself to major figures such as Sándor Petőfi, Endre Ady, Miklós Radnóti, Sándor Weöres and many others. He enjoyed a particularly warm personal and professional relationship with Weöres. More recently, he contributed new versions of contemporary Hungarian poetry to the anthology *At the End of the Broken Bridge* (2005), for which the present author also received commissions. That Morgan is still active at the age of eighty-six is remarkable in view of the cancer with which he was diagnosed some five years ago, though unfortunately he was too frail to attend the launch of the anthology at the University of Strathclyde.

Let's take the red Budapest poster. Did Edwin Morgan engage with Hungarian poetry to get to know that culture or to get away from his own? I suggest that he intended to absorb Hungary but not to break with Scotland; indeed, he has consistently stressed what he sees as common to both cultures. There are two aspects to this. First, in interviews with Hungarian scholars (eg, in Nagy 1998), he has drawn attention to the fact that both Scotland and Hungary have lived in the shadow of powerful neighbours. He has not needed to add that the cultures of both countries remain a mystery to the rest of Europe: the Scots and the Hungarians, for good and ill, are perceived as exotic. Second, Morgan was attracted to Attila József largely because he found in him a fellow city-poet. The two have in common a strong interest in the deployment of the imagery of the metropolis. Morgan has admitted that József's Budapest poetry may have influenced his own Glasgow poetry. But he has also paid tribute to a poet nearer home, the Scottish-born Victorian poet James Thomson, the author of the long poem *The City of Dreadful Night*, first published in 1874. Thomson evokes a dream vision of an archetypically alienated and alienating city, an urban nightmare of a kind that was to become more familiar during the post-Freudian twentieth century. Morgan writes of this poem:

[The city of dreadful night] becomes simply […] any city that is very large and very old, it has huge buildings, great bridges, squares, cathedrals, mansions, slums, endless streetlamps. Since it is night [in the poem], the streets are relatively empty, but because it is a large city there are plenty of shadowy nocturnal wanderers who are the inhabitants of the place and the actors of the poem – the outcasts of daytime society, the tramps, the drunks, the drug-addicts, the half-crazed, the homeless, the sleepless, the lonely. The poem emphasises the isolation of all these characters: they murmur to themselves, they creep about wrapped up in their own thoughts, they appear as products of a dehumanising process in society which is becoming so competitive it has no room for failure; there are also of course psychological weaknesses which are not being blamed on society, but they too take their place within the parameters that society sets up, and the individual seems able to do less and less to change his condition.

(Thomson, 1993: 24)

Much in that comment could be applicable equally to the urban poetry of Morgan and József, especially the latter. József's is a poetry of the exploited proletarian and the mentally disturbed: he himself was both.

Affinities between the two poets can be cited with a certain precision. There is a line in Morgan's poem, 'A View of Things' (Morgan 1985: 45-6) which reads like an echo of József's 'Külvárosi éj' ('Night in the Suburbs'): 'what I hate about decrepit buildings is their reluctance to disintegrate'. Consider these lines from the József poem:

Csönd, – lomhán szinte lábraka
s mászik a súroló kefe;
fölötte egy kis faldarab
azon tünődik, hulljon-e.
(József [nd]: 268)

Morgan translates this as:

Silence. – The scrubbing-brush sluggishly
rises and drags itself about:
above it, a small piece of wall is in
two minds to fall or not.
(József, 2001: 21)

Such images are not uncommon in Hungarian poetry, and this is not surprising if one walks through those parts of Budapest which are unfrequented by tourists. One of the best-known pieces by the contemporary poet Győző Ferencz (b. 1954) offers an example from the last years of the Kádár régime (1956-88):

VIGYÁZAT, OMLÁSVESZÉLY!

Ha épület volnék, most darabokban
Lemállanék rólam a vakolat,
És kiütköznék rajtam, úgy, ahogy van,
A megroggyant váz a felszín alatt: [...]
(Ferencz, 1989: 51)

DANGER, FALLING DEBRIS

If I were a building, chunks of plaster
would now flake off and fall into the street.

from beneath the surface my mauled frame
would stick right out, as it stands in me: [...]
(Ferencz, 1988: 78)

Here the derelict building suggests existential overtones and political undertones.

Morgan's own Glasgow, however, is a city which had a long reputation for some of the worst slums in Europe. The Scottish poet was well placed to respond to the drab city-scapes of Attila József. In the József poem to which reference has just been made, there appears that domestic animal which is most associated with street-wisdom: the cat. The first great poet of the city, Baudelaire, was also the most evocative of feline life. Cats can negotiate city life more skilfully than dogs, though both acquire a certain alertness in such an environment. In Morgan's version of the József poem, 'A View of Things' (József 2001: 21-24), a cat stretches its paw through the railings of a factory fence, and a politically-active working man, distributing illegal leaflets, sniffs like a dog and looks over his shoulder like a cat, to see if the coast is clear. In his sequence of 'Glasgow Sonnets', the eyes of a cat glitter under an abandoned baby-carriage, and an emaciated dog engages in joyless fucking. The implication in both the József and Morgan poems is that human life in large cities has become degraded to the less-than-human, and that people have had to develop the survival skills of the wild. In the Glasgow sonnet following the one with the dog and the cat, a slum landlord makes an illegal bargain with a couple which has five kids and can't afford to reject his offer. Bored teenagers have already stripped the neighbouring houses of anything they can lay their hands on. Some survive, others don't. (Morgan 1985: 78-9)

Attila József (1905-1937) is one of the most celebrated, most necessary poets of Hungary. His mother, who was abandoned by his father, took in other people's washing for a living. His early life was spent in a series of odd jobs, and his experiences lent his poetry its authentically 'proletarian' tone and content. He entered the University of Szeged but was expelled for his poetry, which was deemed to be subversive: one of the professors declared that he should not be allowed to teach in any Hungarian school. His statue now stands, in determined pose, in front of the main university building; at the other side of the square can be seen one of the most wildly eccentric examples of *art nouveau* architecture, the Ungar-Mayer House, but József's own life never knew such opulence. He joined the Communist Party but was expelled for his pioneering attempts to fuse Marxist socio-economics with Freudian psychology. Isolated, and afflicted himself with deep psychological problems, he committed suicide in a Lake Balaton resort by throwing himself in front of a train.

I find Morgan's translations of Hungarian poetry far more interesting than references to matters Magyar in his own poetry. The best-known example of the latter is his 'Siesta of a Hungarian Snake', where the poet has fun with the consonants s, sz, zs, and z (Morgan 1985: 17). We can smile, then pass on. The image, in 'Rider', of the nineteenth-century nationalist hero Lajos Kossuth taking 'a coalblack horse from Debrecen' and clattering 'up Candleriggs into the City Hall' doesn't offer any insights into Kossuth's actual speaking tour of Scotland in 1856 (Morgan, 1985: 72). Perhaps that is a literal-minded response on my part, but the poet's attempt to be surreal is too self-conscious. In my view, Morgan is not at his best when he is being modishly (and somewhat pretentiously) allusive: easy fodder, no doubt, for literary Glasgow in its most self-congratulatory mode. Morgan deserves better than the city's piety towards him.

More productively we can turn to the third question posed on the Rákoczi Street posters: 'Did you travel here to get to know the customs or to do something uncustomary?' Clearly (and despite the gimmickry just mentioned) Morgan's engagement with Hungarian culture is a serious one. However, given the preconceptions of 'exoticism' suffered by Hungarian literature and the language in which it is composed, Morgan's active interest in the country's poetry might seem to many to be 'uncustomary'. Yet there were Scottish precedents. Hugh MacDiarmid – whose poetry has been the object of some of Morgan's most percipient literary criticism – did not himself attempt any versions of Hungarian poetry, but he wrote in defence of the position of Endre Ady (1877-1919) in European modernism. For MacDiarmid, Ady was one of a number of major figures, from 'peripheral' European cultures, 'those, untranslated into English/ For lack of whom the perspective of poetry/ In that language is hopelessly inadequate' ('In Memoriam James Joyce', in MacDiarmid 1978: 820). One might add that an ignorance of European culture renders a perspective on Scottish literature 'hopelessly inadequate', but there are few in Scottish literary academia who are listening. The poets, as usual, are well ahead of the academics. Two twentieth-century Scottish poets, both associates of MacDiarmid, actually went ahead and turned poems by Ady into – Scots! William Soutar (1898-1943) turned Ady's 'Sem utódja, sem boldog őse' into his 'I Lang to Gie Mysel" (Soutar 1988: 319) and Sydney Goodsir Smith (1915-75)'s 'Alane wi the Sun' derives from the Hungarian's 'Egyedül a tengerrel' (Smith 1950: 11). These are both extremely free renderings of the Ady poems. This is more visually obvious in Smith's version, where he reduces Ady's six stanzas to his own four.

Morgan's approach to translation is very different. He attempts to follow the original as closely as he can, and is especially concerned to retain its tone. He has stated his principle of 'being a good servant to the foreign poet' (Dósa 2001: 14). Moreover, although Morgan writes very accomplished original poems in Scots, he has remarked that he deliberately opted for English when tackling József; his versions of Ady are also in English. He did say, though, that he 'thought briefly about Scots words for Attila József' (Dosa 2001: 15). I will come back to this fascinating possibility – fascinating to me personally, at any rate – because Scots is now considered a working-class language and of course József's poetry deals strongly with proletarian themes.

The evidence, then, is that a Scot translating József – or any other Hungarian poet – into English or Scots would not be as 'uncustomary' or as 'exotic' as might first appear. What was 'uncustomary', in Morgan's view, was that József was writing an urban poetry of a kind that had not so far been attempted in either English or Scottish poetry – with the exception, of course, of *The City of Dreadful Night*. Moreover, although in our own time there now exist different English versions of many József poems, it was not always so. When Edwin Morgan first became interested in Attila József during the early 1950s, it had not been 'customary' to put him into English. At first knowing no Hungarian, Morgan discovered József's work in a book of Italian translations by Umberto Albini, published in 1952. With the aid of a Hungarian-English dictionary, Morgan duly worked his way through József's œuvre. Eventually he acquired enough of the language to attempt his own English translations of József and of the other Hungarian poets mentioned earlier. There is a curious parallel with the case of the American critic Edmund Wilson, who learned enough Hungarian in order to appreciate Ady, at a time when good English versions of that poet simply did not exist.

By 1985 Morgan's reputation as a translator of Hungarian poetry was well-established in Hungary itself, and in that year he was presented with the Soros Translation Award for his work on József. In 2001 these poems were conveniently collected in a slim volume from the Glasgow-based small press, Mariscat. The book includes a version of the particular poem ('Tiszta szívvel') which led to József's expulsion from the University of Szeged, here under the title of 'Heart-Innocent'. It opens thus:

Without father, without mother, alone
without cradle, without shroud I go
without God, without land and home
without kiss, without girl to know [...]
(József, 2001: 11)

Morgan has commented on how the work of a foreign poet has revealed itself to him before he has actually 'understood' it. For example, he writes of a poem by the Italian poet Eugenio Montale: 'his world stirs and reveals itself [...] there is a shimmer, a play of light on water and on crumbling buildings [that image again! – TH], a face glancing in a mirror, an accordion being played in the twilight [....]' (quoted in McCarey, nd) It is if there is an ur-poem beyond the actual words, an essence that one can appreciate in a 'deverbalised' condition. This idea derives ultimately from Walter Benjamin, but the eminent translator and former President of the Hungarian Republic, Árpád Göncz, has written of "the charm of half understood words' which every translator knows,' (Göncz 1999: 293), and one could point also to the stages in a text where, according to Wolfgang Iser, the reader must negotiate 'indeterminacy' – the 'gaps' and 'blanks' in that text.

Such is the beginning of the process of engagement between Morgan and József. As for the end-products, what we find in both poets - in Morgan's own poetry at its considerable best and in his versions of József – is a poetry of struggle as opposed to a poetry of contentment, a poetry for alert citizens rather than for passive consumers.

Edwin Morgan told my Miskolc University colleague, Dr Attila

Dósa, that the József poems which probably moved him most were those on the poet's mother, the overworked and terminally ill laundress (Dósa 2001: 12). He therefore tried hard to make a good translation of 'Mama', and under the title of 'Mother' it appears on page 10 of the Mariscat volume. He judges it artistically desirable, in stanza 2, to depart from the rhyme-scheme of the original, replacing *ccdd* with *cdcd*. The mother hangs up the clothes in the attic to dry, and here both Morgan opts for a cold northern climate – 'flying in the wind' – which is not emphasised by other translators of the poem, except for myself in my reference to 'the brisk air' in my forthcoming Scots version. I wanted to turn in a decidedly Scottish poem, and I suspect that Morgan, consciously or otherwise, is doing the same. As for the last two lines of the poem, Morgan reverses their order. 'szürke haja lebben az égen,/ kékítőt old az ég vizében' becomes 'The wet sky shines washed with her blue,/ her grey hair streams where the clouds scud through.' (József 2001: 10) Morgan seeks to preserve the tone, according to his translation policy, but he is prepared – quite acceptably in my view – to make other changes in order to arrive at a readable poem in English. Interestingly, his tenth Glasgow sonnet closes with an image of the women of the slums carrying their washing: '[...] and when they trudge/ from closemouth to laundrette their steady shoes/ carry a world that weighs us like a judge.' (Morgan, 1985: 82) This reads like an echo of the József poem.

As for 'Reménytelenül' – 'Without Hope' in József 2001: 48 – John Bátki (József 1973: 16) has cited a critical consensus which sees this poem as a response to József's expulsion from the Communist Party and his increasing isolation and existential anxiety. It is not one of the 'city' poems but if anything it is much bleaker. More than other translators of the poem, Morgan is faithful to the *abab* rhyme scheme. None of the versions, however, can convey the possible echo of Ferenc Kölcsey's 'Hymnusz' in stanza 1, line 3. Kölcsey's 1823 poem provided the words of the national anthem and is therefore known to every Hungarian. The action of looking around and not finding hope can never have the same resonance in English (or Scots) as it will in Hungarian. This is a culturally-specific detail that cannot be carried over into another language, and there is no point in trying to find equivalences where they simply don't exist.

During the preparation of this paper I decided to attempt my own Scots versions, as I felt I could not adequately grasp Morgan's strategies unless I found my own way of getting into the guts of the poems. In stanza 2 both Morgan and I avoid the 'nyárfa' (poplar). I cannot speak for Morgan, but I saw the poplar as a south-European tree and therefore out of place in the north-European poem which I was trying to make; again I can only speculate that Morgan may have made a similar decision at that point.

Finally, if Morgan offers us a József filtered through a Glasgow and west of Scotland sensibility, I, as an easterner, have positioned my version in my native county of Fife. For decades our main heavy industry was coal, and many of the pits were situated near the sea. Even today the sand on the beach is mingled with coal-dust. Both my grandfathers were miners, so I had a close personal interest in attempting to evoke the proletarian flavour of József's poetry. In south Fife, not only ex-coalminers but working men generally address each other as 'sir'. The word doesn't have the sense of deference that we find in its standard English contexts; in Fife Scots it's a form of address between equals. To call your workmate 'sir' implies male bonding, but there's also more than a hint of mockery – proletarian banter, if you like, for example as in 'Ay, ay, sir, wha wis that lassie I saw ye wi last nicht?' So I opted for this usage in the first line of my (again forthcoming) version. In the József poem, however, the banter is much darker than in the example which I have just given. The Scots and the Hungarians are both famous for their pessimism, and I would suggest that in both our cultures the sense of humour is as blackly ironic as it's possible to be. Attila József has a reputation as a gloomy poet, but that is hardly inconsistent with the grim smile which he wears throughout his work. That in itself is surely attractive to Scottish poet-translators. Sometimes an artistic 'diaspora' works out as a way of travelling not so much hopefully as homefully.

WORKS CITED:

Dósa, Attila (2001). 'A Conversation with Edwin Morgan', *Poetry Review*, 91/3: 8-15.
Ferencz, Győző (1988). 'Danger, Falling Debris', translated by Gerard Gorman and the author, *The Hungarian PEN*, no. 29: 78.
Ferencz, Győző (1989). *Omlásveszély*. Budapest: Szépirodalmi Könyvkiadó.
Göncz, Árpád (1999). *In Mid-Stream: Talks & Speeches*. Budapest: Corvina.

Hubbard, Tom (2006). 'Scottish-Hungarian Literary Connections: Past, Present and Possible Future', in Zsuzsanna Rawlinson, ed., *HUSSE Papers 2005: Proceedings of the Seventh Biennial Conference*, Veszprém: Hungarian Society for the Study of English: 13-26.

József, Attila (nd) *Osszes versei és müfordításai*. [Budapest:] Cserépfalvi.

József, Attila (1973). *Selected Poems and Texts*. Translated from the Hungarian by John Bátki. Cheadle: Carcanet.

József, Attila (2001). *Sixty Poems*. Translated by Edwin Morgan. Glasgow: Mariscat Press.

McCarey, Peter (nd) 'Edwin Morgan the Translator', at http://www.thesyllabary.com/8EdwinM.htm

McClure, J. Derrick (2000). 'William Soutar's Theme and Variation: the Gamut of Literary Translation', in Susanne Hagemann, ed., *Terranglian Territories: Proceedings of the Seventh International Conference on the Literature of Region and Nation*. Frankfurt am Main: Peter Lang: 141-159.

MacDiarmid, Hugh (1978). *Complete Poems 1920-1976*. Edited by Michael Grieve and W R Aitken. 2 vols. London: Martin Brian & O'Keeffe.

Morgan, Edwin (1985). *Selected Poems*. Manchester: Carcanet.

Morgan, Edwin (1996). *Collected Translations*. Manchester: Carcanet.

Nagy, Enikő (1998). 'Moving Crystal Mountains: Edwin Morgan and George Szirtes Talk About Translating Hungarian Poetry', *The AnaChronist*. Budapest: ELTE Department of English Studies: 281-294.

Smith, Sydney Goodsir (1950). 'Alane wi the Sun: from Endre Ady', *Scottish Art and Letters*.

Soutar, William (1988). *Poems of William Soutar: a New Selection*. Edited by W R Aitken. Edinburgh: Scottish Academic Press.

Thomson, James (1993). *The City of Dreadful Night*. Introduced by Edwin Morgan. Edinburgh: Canongate.

Turczi, István, ed. (2005). *At the End of the Broken Bridge: XXV Hungarian Poems 1978-2002*. Manchester: Carcanet.

Wandering Scots: Home and Abroad

In Scotland – and out of it – we have two groups of writers: those who live in mainland Europe or beyond and reflect on the native land, and those who are based in Scotland and work with a European accent of the mind. Naturally these two groups mesh into one another (for example, there are the temporary expats with more than one 'sense of belonging', or none). The Scottish poets Alastair Reid (1926-2014) and Kenneth White (b. 1936) had wandered far from Scotland, but both would make appearances there from time to time – the return of the native. Alastair Reid came from Whithorn in the far south-west of Scotland but lived, since World War Two, in Spain, Switzerland, the USA, and the Dominican Republic, not far from the spot where Christopher Columbus landed. In his prose book *Whereabouts: Notes on Being a Foreigner* (1987), Reid discusses the Spanish word *escueto*. It currently means 'spare, undecorated, stark'. But he looked it up in an etymological dictionary and found that the word had been used to describe people who went on pilgrimages, such as the Scots. This dictionary gave meanings such as 'free', 'uncomplicated', 'unencumbered', 'without luggage'. Probably, Reid goes on, these pilgrims would carry for food only a small bag of oatmeal. He says: 'The word absorbed me, for it is clearly a *Spanish* notion, or translation, of the Scottish character – a view from outside, which chooses to interpret Scottish frugality as a freedom rather than a restraint. It was just the word for the transition I was then making. In Scotland, I had felt cumbered; in Spain, I was learning to be *escueto*, unencumbered.' (*Whereabouts*, 1987, p. 33-34)

Reid had felt oppressed by the joylessness, the narrowness, the sheer negativity of Scottish small-town life. The legacy of Calvinism was still strong. When he was a young boy, an uncle from the Cocos Islands stirred his curiosity for faraway lands. Young Reid was living with his parents in the Borders town of Selkirk. He recalls one local worthy remarking that 'a day oot o Selkirk is a day wastit' ('Borderlines', in *Memoirs of a Modern Scotland*, ed. Karl Miller, 1970, p. 155). Local people resented those who had gone away in search of a richer, more fulfilling existence. If the strays came back to visit, the stay-at-homes would regard them suspiciously – 'You've been away' ('Borderlines', p. 156). As a young man Reid went to university at St Andrews, that ancient city with its ruined cathedral, and its decayed (but hardly ruined) academics. A poem recalls an incident from Reid's student days, an incident that seemed to sum up the Scots' guilty feelings about beauty; he was enjoying a rare day of glorious weather:

> [...] Walking into town, I saw, in a radiant raincoat,
> the woman from the fish-shop. ' What a day it is!'
> cried I, like a sunstruck madman.
> And what did she have to say for it?
> Her brow grew bleak, her ancestors raged in their graves
> as she spoke with their ancient misery:
> 'We'll pay for it, we'll pay for it, we'll pay for it!'

('Scotland', in *Weathering: Poems and Translations*, 1978, p. 39)

A psychiatrist friend told Reid that if Sigmund Freud 'had known anything about Scotland, he would have left Vienna like an arrow and taken on the whole [Scottish] population as a collective patient, to treat the national neurosis, the compulsive-obsessive rigidity that permeates its population.' (*Whereabouts*, p. 26) I myself have often felt that if there were a Nobel Prize for Guilt, it would always be won by a Scot.

Well, Reid got out, and felt his very personality changing as he became more fluent in another language – Spanish. He became less inhibited, more exuberant. He used gestures, spoke with his hands. He had discovered another culture; he had discovered another self.

Reid is both wanderer and wonderer; he has written several poems about cats, about their roving ways, their relentless curiosity, their contrast with dogs (and with most Scots?) who are contentedly domestic. Reid clearly identifies with cats.

And yet cats do come home, even if eventually they go off again. For Reid, 'roots' are not a favourite metaphor: he prefers to talk of 'a web, a web of people and places' (*Whereabouts*, p.65). He remembers a corridor in his parents' house: at one end was his father's study – his father was a church minister – and at the other end was the kitchen, his mother's domain. On one of his return journeys, he made a pilgrimage to this manse (our word for a clergyman's house) and found that the corridor, which had seemed so endless when he was a child, was now actually quite short. The Austro-German poet Rainer Maria Rilke experienced similar feelings when he paid a brief visit to his native Prague – the buildings seemed to have shrunk, and he felt sorry for them. Yet there was nothing smugly patronising about Reid's attitudes when he would come back temporarily to Scotland; his tone is amused, buoyant, affectionate even, without being sentimental. There is a moving account of him standing between his father – who stayed – and his son – to whom Scotland was a new experience, as all three are present on the platform at St Boswells' railway station. Steam chuffs out of the train, and Alastair feels that he is simultaneously a son and a father. The steam clears, and the moment passes with it.

In a poem 'The Manse' he returns to a childhood home to find that it's been demolished, but he is rather glad that this discovery has averted his feelings of nostalgia (*Weathering*, p. 16-17). In another poem, 'The Spiral', we discern the sensibility of a man who travels as much in time as in space: the poet is moving house, and he is therefore leaving forever a place which contained so much of his life.

> [...] The present is a devious wind
> obliterating days and promises.
> Tomorrow is a tinker's guess. [...]

A few lines on he situates this moment as part of a general pattern in his life.

> For possibility,
> I choose to leave behind
> each language, each country. [...]

The poem concludes with the three-generations motif, here modulated but poignantly complementary to the instance at St Boswells, cited above.

> Across the spiral distance,
> through time and turbulence,
> the rooted self in me
> maps out its true country.
>
> And, as my father found

his own small weathered island,
so will I come to ground

where that small man, my son,
can put his years on.

For him, too, time will turn.

(*Weathering*, p. 77-78)

Reid went on to become a distinguished poet and translator. He befriended Jorge Luis Borges and Pablo Neruda and has made superb English versions of their work and that of other Latin American writers. Neruda would ask Alastair to recite the work of MacDiarmid to him. When Neruda died at his Chilean home in 1973, shortly after Pinochet's right-wing coup, Alastair wrote an eloquent poem in memoriam. He claims that in *Las alturas de Machu Picchu*, Neruda became the poet not only of his country but of his continent. It's difficult to imagine a single poet who could write for the whole of Europe.

Reid translated the whole of Neruda's *Isla Negra*; here is his version of 'Exilio' ('Exile') from that long poem:

Exile is round in shape,
A circle, a ring.
Your feet go in circles, you cross land
And it's not your land.
Light wakes you up and it's not your light.
Night comes down, but your stars are missing.
You discover brothers, but they're not of your blood.
You're like an embarrassed ghost,
not loving more those who love you so much,
and it's still so strange to you that you miss
the hostile prickles of your own country,
the loud helplessness of your own people,
the bitter matters waiting for you
that will be snarling at you from the door.

(Pablo Neruda, *Isla Negra*, 1982, p. 233, 235)

I'll return later to this question of exile, to that uneasy question of what is 'home'. Meanwhile, we may focus on a second Scottish poet who has chosen to live abroad. He comes from the western, Atlantic seaboard of Scotland to the western, Atlantic seaboard of Brittany, and was formerly Professor of Poetry at the Sorbonne; he leads a movement for what he calls *geopoetics*. This is Kenneth White, who believes that the 'intellectual nomad' leaves history behind in favour of geography. I'm sceptical. I feel this is too close to the once conventional wisdom that history ended in 1989. One could argue that the opposite is the case, that history in the 1990s and beyond has in fact unfrozen in a way that challenges the West as much as the East; in this regard the events of 11th September 2001 were not so much world-changing (according to the cliché) as the confirmation of existing tendencies. When White thinks of West and East he thinks rather of Celtic Zen – a meeting-point of Gaelic and Buddhist sensibilities. Much in this is certainly very stimulating, and it undoubtedly clears the mind to wander the sea-shore, like White in his poetry, meditating on gulls and rocks. Hugh MacDiarmid recognised this – and more profoundly – in his writings on the East-West synthesis and in his long poem 'On a Raised Beach'. (Actually, rocks, and the sea, are recurrent in Scottish poetry: rocks have a fixity, the sea is in movement and seemingly endless. There you have an image of home [the rocks] – and abroad [the sea].

Yes, to clear the mind is both refreshing and necessary but clearing also involves emptying. I'm not sure that empty minds will respond healthily to the challenges of Europe and the world in the new millennium. In an early critique of White's work, Michael Hamburger questioned the Scotsman's negative attitude to urban life. Hamburger suggested that White 'shows little awareness of the greed and cruelty of nature, or of the very great difficulties that arise in any attempt to derive models for human existence from non-human nature alone.' (Michael Hamburger, *The Truth of Poetry: Tensions in Modern Poetry from Baudelaire to the 1960s*, 1982, p. 297). Hamburger posited rather ideas of 'the Good City' as a complement to the non-human and the cosmic. For the poet Edwin Muir in 1948, 'The Good Town' was something very different from the impersonal metropolis, whether that be slum-ridden Glasgow or totalitarian Prague. He had had too much experience of both. His model was *pre-war* Prague, with its easy-going contact between writers such as Karel Čapek and everyday people: 'it was the first thing that made me wish that Edinburgh might become a similar place.' (Muir, *An Autobiography*, 1964, p. 189) It was during his first residence in Prague that Muir experienced a reawakening, even a rebirth; shortly after, he started to write poetry, at the age of thirty-five. A *human* community had encouraged this, not rocks and gulls.

The poems 'The Good Town' and 'The Labyrinth' record Muir's anguish when Prague had again become the city of Kafka's nightmares. (Muir, *Collected Poems* 1960, 183-6, 163-5). Let's retrace these seventy-plus years since the Stalinist putsch in Czechoslovakia and return to White. Like Reid, he enjoys some creative etymology; for White, the words 'Scot' and 'Scythian' come from the same word *sgeithte*, wanderers. (White, *On Scottish Ground*, 1998, p. 29) He claims that he is reviving the tradition of *Scotus vagans*, the wandering Scot, which goes back to Scottish monks traversing Europe from Galway to Prague (White, 'The Wandering Scot', *ArtWork*, April / May 1983, p. 4-5); George Buchanan lecturing at Bordeaux and Coimbra in Portugal; Sir Thomas Urquhart of Cromarty, who translated Rabelais into idiosyncratic English and who died, according to White, 'at the age of about sixty/ suddenly/ on the continent/ in a fit of excessive laughter'; Michael Scot 'the leading mind in western Europe/ in the early thirteenth century/ an *'internationalgebildeter Mann'* .' (White, *Open World: the Collected Poems 1960-2000*, 2003, p. 164-5, 170 and *passim* in White's work) We can be grateful to Kenneth White for drawing our attention to these figures. I'm particularly keen on Michael Scot, who competes with the fictional Dr Jekyll for the title of Scottish Faust. Scot was (according to tradition) born in Balwearie Tower, a couple of miles from where I live; I often walk there. Dante consigned Scot to his *Inferno*, which I suppose has received all Fausts, Scottish and otherwise. I tried to redress the balance when I wrote a comic ballad on the legend of Michael Scot's outwitting the devil – Scot challenged him to make a rope out of the sand on the sea-shore of Kirkcaldy. (Hubbard, *The Chagall Winnocks*, 2011, pp 3-4)

So we're back to sea-shores. If I've seemed unduly harsh on Kenneth White, I'd like to counter that by citing a musical tribute to him by Ronald Stevenson (1928-2015), a Scottish composer, international concert pianist, and a leading authority on the music and writings of Ferruccio Busoni, the Italo-German composer of *Doktor Faust*. This is Stevenson's *String Quartet: Voces Vagabundae*

– 'Voices of the Vagabonds' of 1990. The second movement, a
vivid scherzo, is subtitled 'The Bird Path: homage to the Glasgow-
born poet Kenneth White'. (Stevenson / Bodorová, *String Quartets*,
CD, Praha, 2003) It was in 1989 and 1990, when the poet had his
first cordial encounter with Stevenson, that White's work began to
be noticed and published in his native Scotland; for the previous
twenty years he was published mainly in his adopted France.

Kenneth White would deny that he is an escapist. 'You don't lose
roots', he says, 'you just realise they go further than people think.'
(White, 'The Wandering Scot', p. 5) Like Alastair Reid he found
Scotland constricting and needed a wider field for his Scottish
energy. Certainly Scotland has become remote, for reasons not only
of geography but also of history. There are many Scots, at home
and abroad, who are working hard, often behind the scenes, to
change that. Some of our livelier minds, though, might be forgiven
for wondering, even if only now and then, why they should remain
in Scotland. As a gloss on Alastair Reid's remarks on Selkirk, I
relish White's quotation from a church minister's prayer: 'O Lord,
bless and be gracious to the Greater and the Lesser Cumbraes and
in thy mercy do not forget the adjacent islands of Great Britain
and Ireland.' (*On Scottish Ground*, p. 151).

In my view Kenneth White lacks a troubled tension with his
native land. He goes back to Glasgow and Edinburgh but writes
of them as a self-consciously enlightened outsider, without Reid's
still deeply emotional response to what *he* left behind.

I want now to consider a number of writers in whom that
tension is particularly strong, forbidding them the superior tone
which I feel mars so much of White's work.

The poet Tessa Ransford (1938-2015) has in effect made
a journey the reverse of that of Kenneth White; he has gone
mentally from West to East, she has come physically from East to
West. Ransford was born in India, where her father was in charge
of the Royal Mint.

> I was a baby in India
> born among dark eyes and thin limbs
> handled by slim fingers
> bounced by bangles
> and held high among the turbans [...]

(Ransford, *Light of the Mind*, 1980, p. 9)

Back in Scotland, she discovered Europe. It is notable that so many Scottish poets of international outlook (not least Hamish Henderson) have been drawn to Rilke, that perpetual wanderer. Ransford studied German at Edinburgh University and was taught by the eminent Rilke scholar Eudo Mason. He had hoped that she would pursue formal research after graduating, but she felt she must decline; he burst into tears. However, she effectively honoured Mason by maintaining an active love of Rilke, and one of her finest pieces is a version of a Rilke poem, of which here are the first and last verses:

Since delight has winged you
over countless previous precipices,
engineer bold bridges now
whose arching defies geometries.

[...]

Let your practised skills outreach
until they join wide contraries,
for within the limits of human touch
the god discovers his mysteries.

('Since Delight has Winged You', in *Sonnet Selection, with eight Rilke lyrics translated*, 2007, p. 25)

Late in her career she visited the former East Germany and the outcome was an anthology, edited and translated by her, *The Nightingale Question: 5 Poets from Saxony* (2004).

Like Tessa Ransford, J F Hendry (1912-86) lived in other continents, and was able to offer a creatively oblique perspective to the Scottish scene. A professional translator and linguist, he worked in Vienna, Brussels and in Toronto, and wrote an essay on contemporary Scottish poetry, 'Inside the Ghetto' (*Chapman* magazine, no. 20, 1977), that wittily and waspishly challenged the cosy domestic critical consensus, as he saw it. In his collection *A World Alien* (1980) he has some sombre, expressionistic poems on his native Glasgow. His biography of Rilke, *The Sacred Threshold* (1983), perhaps hints at his own ambivalence towards his native land. Discussing the Prodigal Son sequence in Rilke's *Notebooks of*

Malte Laurids Brigge, Hendry identifies the Prodigal Son, Malte, and Rilke with each other. 'Their journeys are more and more in the nature of flights, and they long for a home.' (p. 79) The Prodigal finds that his family forgive him – but they fail to understand his mission. Hendry often felt that he himself was misunderstood in Scotland. He points out that Rilke, a Praguer by birth, knew the Czech folk song 'Kde Domův Muj' ('Where is My Home'), 'and this could have fuelled his pride in being homeless.' (p. 22) If Rilke and Hendry were in any sense Czech or Scottish, how much more were they European; their responses to their origins had to be complex and contradictory.

Writers from eastern Scotland have a special regard for mainland Europe: the next landfall beyond our coast is Scandinavia. George Bruce (1909-2002) writes of his native Buchan, of a promontory rising towards Norway. Scotland is a country of so many small islands, although we have fewer of them on the east. It is not surprising that Ulysses, Odysseus, that island wanderer, makes many appearances in Scottish poetry from MacDiarmid through George Campbell Hay to Alastair Mackie. Mackie (1925-95), an Aberdonian by birth, lived on the coast of Fife, on the North Sea. In his 'Back-Green Odyssey', Mackie counterpoints the desire to travel with the desire to stay at home. His is a comic, anti-heroic persona, the schoolteacher who steers his boat 'sittin on my doup-end'. He sits on a chair in his back garden, looking out to the harbour and the sea. This is 'tethert vaigin' – tethered travelling. His Penelope is his wife hanging out the clothes to dry. 'Me Odysseus?' he asks with rhetorical self-mockery. Certainly not; his friend Hugh MacDiarmid was much more like the old Greek. Mackie juxtaposes his Scots translations of Ulysses poems by du Bellay, Mallarmé, Valéry, Umberto Saba, calling on these other voices to help him explore the contradictions of home and abroad. 'A herbour is a tension atween twa pulls/ the beck o horizons and the rug o hame.' (Mackie, *Collected Poems 1954-1994*, 2012, p. 205) The word 'gangrel' (a wanderer, a vagrant) was a favourite of an older Scottish poet, Sydney Goodsir Smith (1915-75); Mackie applies the concept to Odysseus. Yet stay-at-home Mackie is in a sense an intellectual gangrel or wanderer by the very act of putting his Scots verse in intimate dialogue with the French and Italian poets. He tacitly Europeanises his Scots utterance.

It is this cultural dialogue, with Europe and the world, which the wandering Scots have to sustain and develop. In doing so we enrich not only our own threatened cultures but also our sister cultures elsewhere. Richard Demarco (b. 1930) is an Italo-Scottish artist and former gallery director who believes passionately in Scottish-international dialogue. He calls his quest 'the road to Meikle Seggie', a road which takes us by way of the Cyclades and the Hebrides. (Demarco, *The Road to Meikle Seggie*, 1978, new edition 2015, *passim*) Meikle Seggie is the name of a farm north of Milnathort, but in a symbolic sense, the road to Meikle Seggie *doesn't* exist on a map, as if we neither can nor should reach that place; for Robert Louis Stevenson, of whom Demarco is an ardent admirer, it's the journey that counts, rather than the destination. Demarco has organised expeditions which take in equally the old drover roads of Scotland and places of tragic pilgrimage in Poland and Romania.

As Hugh MacDiarmid put it so well in his long poem *In Memoriam James Joyce* (1955), and if we could take on the word 'international' as well as 'intranational':

And rejoicing in all those intranational differences which
Each like a flower's scent by its peculiarity sharpens
Appreciation of others as well as bringing
Appreciation of itself, as experiences of gardenia or zinnia
Refine our experience of rose or sweet pea.

Writing Scottishly on Non-Scottish Matters

> He was one of that class of rovers you sometimes meet at
> sea, who never reveal their origin, never allude to home, and
> go rambling over the world as if pursued by some mysterious
> fate they cannot possibly elude.

That is how, in Herman Melville's *Typee*, the narrator introduces his
fellow-sailor Toby, a diminutive, supple fellow who has the air of
a 'strange, wayward being, moody, fitful, and melancholy - at times
almost morose.' Melville's œuvre is notable for its many 'isolatos' –
most famously, the narrator of *Moby Dick* ('Call me Ishmael') and
that doyen of alienated office-workers, Bartleby. To every call for
him to engage with society's norms, Bartleby offers the ostinato
reply: 'I would prefer not to'.

The 'isolato' is a literary archetype akin to the Wandering Jew,
who is so pervasive in Western cultural tradition. The Wandering
Scot surely belongs here. The Edinburgh-born Robert Louis
Stevenson was an admirer of Melville, and that shows in the
Scottish writer's later work set in the south Pacific. However, it's in
The Master of Ballantrae, a novel from 1889 set variously in Scotland,
France, India and north America that Stevenson offers his own
brand of the 'isolato' - 'a strange, wayward being' subject to destiny
or circumstances, and fuses it with the 'Wandering Scot', a figure
who feels obliged to leave Scotland for political, economic or even
cultural reasons. The eponymous Master of Ballantrae, aka James
Durie, is a man of sterling qualities who never succeeds in his
most cherished ambitions in Scotland or anywhere else for that
matter. Yet the failures of this charismatic, arrogant and even evil
fellow lead him to a tragic grandeur that's seemingly unattainable
by his dully virtuous brother, Henry, who efficiently manages the
family's estate. Not for James Durie the predictable life of a stay-
at-home, of a bureaucrat with limited horizons. 'I know the world,'
he says, 'as few men know it when they come to die – court and
camp, the east and the west; I know where to go, I see a thousand
openings. I am now at the height of my resources, sound of health,
of inordinate ambition. Well, all this I resign; I care not if I die and
the world never hear of me; I care only for one thing, and that I
will have.' He then issues a cold threat to his interlocutor, the old

family servant Ephraim Mackellar: 'Mind yourself, lest when the roof falls, you, too should be crushed under the ruins.'

James Durie, Master of Ballantrae, is to my mind Stevenson's greatest creation, a compound of Milton's Satan and Goethe's Mephistopheles, and at the same time a pre-modernist example of the precariously-proceeding existential anti-hero, staking everything at each critical moment that calls for a choice: will he take this course of action, or that one? Perversely, and with supreme contempt for the negotiations by which most people get through their lives, he paradoxically chooses not choice but chance – he'll let his path be decided by the toss of a coin.

James Durie's wanderings take him to France (that spiritual home for Scottish sophisticates), India, and the north American wilderness, in the Adirondacks. Perhaps what is most strikingly Scottish about this homeless expatriate is his origin, substantially, in native folklore. I cited Milton and Goethe but Stevenson's character could well be regarded as a figure from the traditional horror stories which stoked the Scottish writer's imagination from childhood on. The Master of Ballantrae is referred to as a 'warlock' – that wonderful Scots term for a sinister creature, in seemingly human form, who has yet something magnificently of the underworld about him.

As for twenty-first century Scottish novels, I'm intrigued by how one writer in particular recreates imaginatively not the previous century, but the one before that. So to the novel set outside Scotland, with its transposition of space, we might add a further distancing, that of time. The wandering Scot has affinities to the archetype of the Superfluous Man, so pervasive in nineteenth-century Russian fiction and particularly in the work of Ivan Turgenev. The Superfluous Man: this is the guy who just can't fit in; that he spends more time in western Europe than in Russia is both cause and effect of his alienation. But what of the Superfluous Woman? What happens when the isolat*O* is actually an isolat*A*? One method of pursuing such enquiries is to filter them through that sub-genre known in the German-speaking countries as the *Kunstlerroman*: the novel dealing with the development of an artist, and in our specific case a female artist. In an acceptance speech at a prize-giving ceremony for her novel *Clara* (2002), Janice Galloway eschewed any lumpen-feminist reductivism and instead issued a polemic on behalf of all writers – even 'successful' ones

– who struggle to make ends meet. *Clara* is a novel steeped in pan-European history and culture. It imaginatively reconstructs the life of Clara Wieck, the pianist and composer who married Robert Schumann. Society expects that Clara, for all her musical prowess, will remain in the shadow of her famous husband. This she resists, while still striving to be a nurturing mother and carer for Robert as his insanity advances. For all her commitments across Europe as a concert pianist on tour, she clearly has a 'home' to come back to, but the manifold demands on her energies scarcely make 'homecoming' an entirely joyous prospect of deserved warmth and relaxation.

At the time of its appearance, *Clara* seemed to some to be a turning-away from its author's usual 'Scottish' subject-matter. Yet Galloway had earlier produced *Foreign Parts,* a comic masterpiece about culture-clash. Issued in 1994, this novel relates the misadventures of a pair of thirty-something women from the west of Scotland as they attempt to enjoy a holiday in France. *Clara* is still recognisably the work of a writer from Scotland: it's laconic, down-to-earth and contains its fair share of cussing. But there are also numerous allusions to nineteenth-century Germany's (and Europe's) fascination with Scotland, notably as received in the works of Robert Burns and Walter Scott — who both attracted the attention of Austro-German musical practitioners, Robert Schumann among them.

I'd share Galloway's apparent belief – for all her hard-headedness – in the spiritual benefits of art. Writing on Dvořák's opera *The Jacobin,* she called the work 'fresh, full of gorgeous textures and – in the children's choruses at least – simply perfect. In a tale where music is symbolic of human interconnectedness, perhaps it would need to be.' If not quite always, art and the artist can triumph over material contingency, and there's no shortage of material contingency to challenge the protagonist of *Clara.* Interestingly, Ron Butlin, the acclaimed Edinburgh-based writer, has covered territory similar to that of Galloway. In 2004 he brought out *Vivaldi and the Number 3,* an idiosyncratic collection of short stories. Here, mainly nineteenth-century composers are transported to other cultures and even other times. In one of these tales, Dvořák finds transcendent beauty in Czech folklore, turning horrific legends into melodic splendour, as befits that healthiest of composers, an unusual member of a dramatis personae that includes more than its fair share of neurotics and alcoholics. Butlin's realism, while undoubtedly of the magical sort, is also very dark. Beethoven, naïve and bemused in present-day Edinburgh, finds himself in no locus of Galloway's 'human interconnectedness'. What characterises the new millennium, in Scotland as elsewhere, is fragmentation, dumbing-down: 'No primal rhythm moves us any more, only a debased counterpoint of hopes and fears, regrets and self-interest [...] This is the twenty-first century – overlaid by swirling litter, scaffolding and dogshit.' And we fondly imagined Edinburgh to be a world city of literature and culture!

Christopher Harvie's *Dalriada*:
The Condition of Europe

In recent years a curiously recurrent phenomenon has appeared in Scotland: the debut novels by writers in later life, writers distinguished in a field which calls for fact not fiction. Three instances come to mind: such writers are best known as professional historians. Owen Dudley Edwards is the author of *Saint Johnny* (2015), a novel based on the life of St John and reflecting its author's liberal Catholicism; Neal Ascherson, chronicler (and witness) of east-central Europe, has produced *The Death of the Fronsac* (2017), concerning a Polish soldier based in Scotland during the Second World War, and effecting a clear relationship between his historical studies and his art. Our third example is Christopher Harvie's *Dalriada* (2015).

Christopher Harvie (b 1944) is a peripatetic Scot who is Emeritus Professor of British and Irish Studies at the University of Tübingen, maintaining his base in Germany while normally resident in Melrose, not far from Abbotsford, that place of pilgrimage for all admirers of Walter Scott, of which Harvie is one (and a scholastically active one at that). Scott is known as the father of the historical novel, and Christopher Harvie – to whom the boundaries of academic fields are never rigidly demarcated – is aware of how historical fiction blends into its related genre of political fiction. This is the territory of his (so far) only novel.

In many respects it's a companion piece to his work of literary history, *The Centre of Things: Political Fiction in Britain from Disraeli to the Present* (1991). Here he offers a fresh perspective on the so-called 'Condition of England' novels of the early-mid nineteenth century, that cluster of works by Charlotte Brontë, Charles Dickens (*Hard Times* in particular), Benjamin Disraeli, Elizabeth Gaskell and Charles Kingsley. These books afford a rich panorama of the various social classes, their conflicts and such resolutions as appear naïve and fragile to later generations post-Darwin and post-Marx. Harvie would extend the Condition of England genre to later fiction such as Henry James's *The Princess Casamassima* (1886), H G Wells's *Tono-Bungay* (1909) and *The New Machiavelli* (1911). However, he is inclusive of the furthest reaches of these islands, adding to the canon William Alexander's Aberdeenshire novel *Johnny Gibb of*

Gushetneuk (1871) and Charles Kickham's *Knocknagow* (1879), set in County Tipperary: a Condition of Scotland novel, and a Condition of Ireland novel. *Dalriada* is Harvie's own contribution to the former – but it takes in Ireland as well, and mainland Europe, as belonging to a wider field of vision.

A Condition of Scotland novel which is simultaneously a Condition of Europe one? In a review of Ascherson's *The Death of the Fronsac* (*Scottish Review*, March 2018), Harvie regards that work as belonging to the former category and by implication also to the latter. In Ascherson's novel, private lives interact with the public sphere of World War Two; in *Dalriada*, Harvie's microcosmic representatives of the diverse classes are enmeshed in the macrocosm of World War One. (Something of a link with Ascherson's tale of a displaced Pole is discernible towards the end of *Dalriada* when a ship's captain, one Joseph Conrad, makes a cameo appearance in a Glasgow courtroom – it's a comic scene, for sure, but acts as a scherzo for the European motifs of Harvie's symphony.)

In Walter Scott's historical novels there appear actual historical figures alongside their fictional characters. Examples are Rob Roy in the novel of that name and the Young Pretender in *Redgauntlet*. Alexandre Dumas, one of Scott's French disciples, represents the assassination of the real Duke of Buckingham in *The Three Musketeers*, and the lynching of the De Witt brothers in The Hague features in *The Black Tulip*. Napoleon appears in the Waterloo chapter of Stendhal's *The Charterhouse of Parma*. Christopher Harvie follows suit in *Dalriada*: to take the German figures in whom the author – by virtue of his background – would take a special interest, these include Frieda von Richthofen, the wife of D H Lawrence; General Wilhelm Groener; and for good measure, the Austrian novelist Joseph Roth also makes an appearance.

This is a novel which constantly shifts in time and space; put it another way, it's 'a tale which extends over many years and travels into many countries', as Stevenson wrote of his own *The Master of Ballantrae*. *Dalriada* takes the reader from 1914, at the first stirrings of one war, up to 1939, and the outbreak of the next. We're in Scotland's Clydeside with its shipyards, and in Dublin ('Willie Yeats' on the historical moment: 'Things fall apart'), and of course Germany.

Glasgow is of course a major Scottish locus in the novel, with periodic references to its *art nouveau*, Kate Cranston's tearooms, and the City Chambers with 'Mair marble nor the Vatican'. Demotic Scots jostles with the smooth, knowing chatter of the high-heidyins. Christopher Harvie blends Scotland and Germany with more than a hint of parody – 'Siegfried's Journey to the Clyde' – and in a wry allusion to the fictional small state of Gruenewald in Stevenson's German romance *Prince Otto*.

Expansively and resonantly, there is one character's reference to Goethe's visit to Strasbourg Cathedral, a crucial experience in that author's life, and there is the music, with the invocation of Janáček, Sibelius and Nielsen (his Fifth was his wartime symphony) and the legacy of the Austro-German composers. As Harvie wrote in *Mending Scotland: Essays in Economic Regionalism* (2004):

> 'Herr, red' auf mich, dass mein Leben ein Sinn hat'. 'Lord, convince me that my life means something': the great plea of the soloist in Brahms's *German Requiem* is still as rational as its music is glorious. Consolation: the mysticism in religion is still valuable, our presence on this planet being baffling enough; and the legacy of Christianity in music, literature and art is still magnificent, as even fierce critics like MacDiarmid and Larkin would attest. Secular replacements, from Positivism to the current crop of prophylactics, from dieting to astrology, have generally bombed.

He continues:

> Even for the unbeliever, this journey to the heart of the mystery, coupled with the appreciation and intoxication of the tradition – be it the *Book of Kells* or the Bruckner *Te Deum*, the austere cells of the Celtic monks or the treasury of hymns and psalms which remain intriguingly common to both religious traditions – this tradition can recharge resources. If commercialised faith in the USA is probably the nearest we can get to devil-worship, we have to save Christianity from the Christians.

It's a call for us to make our history by means of that which transcends the contingencies of history. *Dalriada* possesses something of what Henry James, writing of Hawthorne's *The House of the Seven Gables*, called 'that vague hum, that indefinable echo of the whole multitudinous life of man, which is the real sign of a great work of fiction.'

Appendix: Scottish Writers on the French, the Russians, and their Writers

JAMES THOMSON ('B.V.') ON STENDHAL (HENRI BEYLE) AND HIS TRAVEL WRITINGS (1875): 'Travelling through the provinces, he declares that 'La Belle France' is as false a title as 'Merry England'. At Marseilles he is invited to dinner, and accepts; but seeing Rossini's 'Semiramide' on the opera-bill he goes with a long face to his inviter, and begs to be excused on the grounds of a splitting headache. Unfortunately that gentleman goes to the opera the same evening, and Beyle's perfidy is discovered. Moral of the ill-treated man: 'Take care never to invite Beyle to dinner on an opera evening.'

ROBERT LOUIS STEVENSON ON ALEXANDRE DUMAS Père (1882): 'Dumas approaches perhaps nearest of any modern to these Arabian [Nights] authors in the purely material charm of some of his romances. The early part of *Monte Cristo*, down to the finding of the treasure, is a piece of perfect story-telling; the man never breathed who shared these moving incidents without a tremor [...] I saw the other day, with envy, an old and very clever lady setting forth on a second or third voyage into *Monte Cristo*. Here are stories which powerfully affect the reader, which can be reperused at any age, and where the characters are no more than puppets.'

MARGARET OLIPHANT ON FRENCH FICTION (1890): 'It occurred to me lately to have a good many conversations with a very intelligent and brilliant Frenchwoman upon this subject. She began, needless to say, by a strenuous protest against the supposition that French novels give any sort of real representation of French life – an opinion which I have always held, partly because I have no belief in the possibility of universal corruption, and partly because domestic life in France has, as it happens, always appeared to me in a very attractive light.'

R B CUNNINGHAME GRAHAM ON GUY DE MAUPASSANT'S 'YVETTE', COMPARING THIS STORY TO G B SHAW'S *MRS WARREN'S PROFESSION* (1898): 'Mrs Warren, being an Englishwoman, was probably sentimental, for sentimentality seems inborn in our race, and cuts us off in a measure both from passion and sentiment. The 'Marquise', on the other hand, was a Latin, and most likely asked no more from life than life could give. [...] Mr Shaw writes powerfully, but with an evident eye to his reader, and loses no opportunity of both preaching and moralising: whereas Maupassant wrote as an artist, and let his readers draw their own conclusions.'

ANDREW LANG ON EDMOND ABOUT'S *LE ROI DES MONTAGNES / THE KING OF THE MOUNTAINS* (1899). [NOTE: About's notorious novel is a satire on nineteenth century Greek life, and on the perceived cosiness of the highland brigands with the authorities in Athens. Hadji Stavros, the 'King of the Mountains' is a ruthless bandit and killer with a large 'staff', and who conducts his enterprise with an air of bourgeois respectability.] 'The peculiarity of Greece was the existence of the extremely modern within four or five miles of the extremely archaic – the robber bands of Hadji Stavros. It was as if the MacDonnells and Camerons had tenanted the Pentlands in the age of David Hume and Lord Monboddo. [...] The grave irony of the King of the Mountains is worthy of Swift: his item of expenditure, 'Repairs of the road to Thebes, which has become impracticable, and where, unfortunately, we found no travellers to rob,' is inimitable. Rob Roy would never have dreamed of repairing the road to Aberfeldy. [...] The fight around the cave, and the attempt to escape by the water-fall, are much in the vein of Stevenson, and do credit to About's versatility.'

GEORGE DOUGLAS BROWN, AUTHOR OF *THE HOUSE WITH THE GREEN SHUTTERS*, TAKES HIS CUE FROM BALZAC (c1902): 'There is a distinct place for incidental psychological sketches in a novel; sometimes you are very familiar with significant traits which, nevertheless, are hardly big enough to make the framework of a whole novel; but if you work them in features of your minor characters these impress by their truth and (if well handled) add to the full conviction of the whole. Balzac has done that with the character of La Fosseuse in *The Country Doctor*.' [It was pointed out long ago that Brown may have found the phrase 'house with the green shutters' in that Balzac novel.]

SCOTTISH WRITERS ON RUSSIA AND ITS WRITERS

THOMAS CARLYLE, IN 1841: 'Yes, truly, it is a great thing for a Nation that it get an articulate voice; that it produce a man who will speak forth melodiously what the heart of it means! Italy, for example, poor Italy lies dismembered, scattered asunder, not appearing in any protocol or treaty as a unity at all; yet the noble Italy is actually one: Italy produced its Dante; Italy can speak! The Czar of all the Russias, he is strong, with so many bayonets, Cossacks and cannons; and does a great feat in keeping such a tract of Earth politically together; but he cannot yet speak. Something great in him, but it is a dumb greatness. He has had no voice of genius, to be heard of all men and times. He must learn to speak. He is a great dumb monster hitherto. His cannons and Cossacks will all have rusted into nonentity, while that Dante's voice is still audible. The Nation that has a Dante is bound together as no dumb Russia can be.'

ROBERT LOUIS STEVENSON READS DOSTOYEVSKY IN FRENCH, 1886 (THE YEAR OF *DR JEKYLL AND MR HYDE*) 'Jekyll is a dreadful thing, I own; but the only thing I feel dreadful about is that damned old business of the war in the members. [...] Raskolnikoff is easily the greatest book I have read in ten years; I am glad you took to it. Many find it dull: Henry James could not finish it: all I can say is, it nearly finished me. It was like having an illness. James did not care for it because the character of Raskolnikoff was not objective; and at that I divined a great gulf between us, and, on further reflection, the existence of a certain impotence in many minds of to-day, which prevents them from living *in* a book or a character, and keeps them standing afar off, spectators of a puppet show. To such I suppose the book may seem empty in the centre; to the others it is a room, a house of life, into which they themselves enter, and are tortured and purified. The Juge d'Instruction I thought a wonderful, weird, touching, ingenious creation: the drunken father, and Sonia, and the student friend, and the uncircumscribed, protaplasmic humanity of Raskolnikoff, all upon a level that filled me with wonder: the execution also, superb in places. Another has been translated – *Humiliés et Offensés*. It is even more incoherent than *Le Crime et le Châtiment*, but breathes much of the same lovely goodness, and has passages of power.'

GEORGE DOUGLAS BROWN, AUTHOR OF *THE HOUSE WITH THE GREEN SHUTTERS* (1901), AND OF SHORT STORIES SET IN RURAL SCOTLAND, ON TURGENEV: 'It was Turgenev's *Sportsman's Sketches* that started me off. I thought I'd try something on similar lines.'

JOHN MACDOUGALL HAY, AUTHOR OF THE EXPRESSIONISTIC NOVEL *GILLESPIE* (1914), AS A READER OF DOSTOYEVSKY'S *THE POSSESSED*: This is less easy to pin down. Over twenty years ago I sat in the National Library of Scotland making notes as I went through Hay's copy of Dostoyevsky's novel, recording those passages which were marked and annotated. I went back to these notes recently, wondering if I could do anything with them, then it occurred to me that the markings might not be by Hay; what if his copy had a previous owner? Unlikely – but there was the nagging doubt. I had evidence – but not proof. If another (and younger!) scholar would like to take this up, please do; comparison of Hay's handwriting in the book with his manuscripts should solve things. It hadn't crossed my mind to do just that at the time. 'The road not taken'.

HUGH MACDIARMID ON TOLSTOY, 1926: 'As Tolstoi o' Lucerne alane / Minded a'e beggar minstrel seen!' These lines from MacDiarmid's *A Drunk Man Looks at the Thistle* immediately follow the poet's reference to Dostoyevsky's encounter with a small girl in a grim part of London. The allusion to Tolstoy is the only one in a poem which makes much more of Dostoyevsky, but it has implications, arguably, for the social consciences of both Tolstoy and MacDiarmid.

For further material on Scottish-Russian literary connections, see Peter McCarey, *Hugh MacDiarmid and the Russians* (1987) and Walter Perrie, *Nietzsche, Dostoyevsky & MacDiarmid's Drunk Man* (2021).

Postscript (2022): An Inexhaustible Quarry

Modern Scottish literature experienced a late coming of age; much of the reason for this was a delayed re-engagement with other literatures of Europe. Elsewhere on our continent, towards the end of the nineteenth century and a little beyond, there was a flurry of 'Young' movements – Young Belgium, Young Poland and so on, with the emergence of writers determined to express new sensibilities and in new forms. To our west, the Irish literary revival got underway with the likes of Yeats, Synge, George Moore and Joyce looking to mainland Europe for the artistic stimuli of the Franco-Belgian Symbolists, of Ibsen and of Wagner. Irish writers went on to mesh these influences with long-dormant native sources, in the identification of the local with the universal which is the antithesis of a cringing provincialism.

During this period, dating roughly from the mid-1880s up to the outbreak of World War One, Scotland knew relatively few of such 'movements': writers operated in isolation, with flashes of a more outward-going spirit in the likes of Robert Louis Stevenson and R B Cunninghame Graham. In the other arts, Charles Rennie Mackintosh was poised to make his mark in the Vienna of 1900; he and his Glasgow-based entourage could indeed be said to form a movement, analogous to the work of Patrick Geddes and his team in the east. However, while RLS was an internationalist in other respects, he did not reciprocate the enthusiasm of Marcel Schwob of the French Symbolists for his own work, possessing as he did a dustily old-fashioned view of French culture and a hearty Presbyterian suspicion of anything that suggested out-and-out decadence. His youthful enthusiasm for Baudelaire was superficial and he piously condemned the French poet for translating an especially lurid tale by Edgar Allan Poe. As it turned out, the Poe-Baudelaire axis would prove itself a major feature of the onset of modernism.

However, it was better that Scotland's cultural revival came late, and in a magnificent manner, than never. Hugh MacDiarmid brought out his long poem *A Drunk Man Looks at the Thistle* in 1926, with its allusions to such as Herman Melville and Dostoevsky, both writers who were undergoing their own revival in the post-war world. MacDiarmid found literary and linguistic models in the work of James Joyce, whose *Ulysses*, along with Proust's *À la recherche du temps perdu* and T S Eliot's *The Waste Land*, marked the culmination of modernism just a few years before *A Drunk Man Looks at the Thistle*.

There would be catch-up, too, in Scottish novels – eventually. The 'big' novels of the nineteenth century, by Balzac, Dickens, Dostoevsky and Zola, which more often than not centred on a young provincial trying to make his mark in the metropolis, found no equivalent in Scotland until Alasdair Gray's 1981 triumph *Lanark*. By that date, the realist and naturalistic modes of fiction had long been succeeded by the magical-realism of Latin America and indeed by surrealism, which found a receptive fictional base in Glasgow, long known for its native off-beat, daft sense of humour. (There's the story, once related by Ludovic Kennedy, of a drunk guy getting on a Glasgow bus and asking the woman sitting opposite: 'Did ye see me gettin oan the bus?' 'Ay' says the wifie. Fella looks sceptical and repeats the question. 'Ay, pal', she insists. 'Ah definitely saw ye. Ye're sittin opposite me.' Drunk then enquires: 'How did ye know it wis me?')

In a 2016 address to the Saltire Society, Kirsty Gunn cautioned against a narrowly prescriptive view of our literary activity, and the bureaucracy-pleasing box-ticking to which it leads. There's a tendency for Scottish writing, and perceptions of Scottish writing, to focus on the worthy, the safely virtuous, to affect a solemnity that isn't the same as seriousness. Such artistic conservatism betrays a provincial insecurity, as if the modern movement had simply by-passed Scotland. Invited to give a keynote lecture at a 'Scotland in Europe' conference at Warsaw University a few years back, I chose to discuss two Scottish novels that were markedly European in ambience and were all the more serious for being hilarious: J David Simons's *The Liberation of Celia Kahn* (2014) concerning the diversity of Jewish attitudes in Glasgow early in the twentieth century, and Fred Urquhart's *Jezebel's Dust* (1951) on Polish soldiers stationed in Edinburgh during World War Two and their sexual encounters with the local girls, not to mention the attendant cultural clashes with the young ladies' families and other insularly-minded Scots.

Literary history teaches us that there are no new stories, but often splendid variations on the old. Such a dialectic animates modernism, but certainly not postmodernism which smugly refuses to acknowledge how the best of the past can help us 'make it new' with depth and resonance. Enter a villainous Dundonian:

> It is clear that [Captain William] Kidd – if Kidd indeed secreted this treasure, which I doubt not – it is clear that he must have had assistance in the labor. But this labor concluded, he may have thought it expedient to remove all participants in his secret. Perhaps a couple of blows with a mattock were sufficient, while his coadjutors were busy in the pit; perhaps it required a dozen – who shall tell?

That concludes 'The Gold Bug', to my mind the most ingenious of Edgar Allan Poe's stories. Certainly, Stevenson needed no Baudelaire as a go-between in order to borrow the essence of 'The Gold Bug' for his own *Treasure Island*; but isn't there something of the metaphor of buried treasure in Hugh MacDiarmid's modernist claims (in 1923) for the Scots language, as here:

> The Scots Vernacular is a vast storehouse of just the very peculiar and subtle effects which modern European literature in general is assiduously seeking [...] The Vernacular is a vast unutilised mass of lapsed observation [...] It is an inchoate Marcel Proust – a Dostoevskian debris of ideas – an inexhaustible quarry of subtle and significant sound.

It's bizarre that a century on we're still expected to issue an apologia for Scots, as if we'd never caught up – have we? – with MacDiarmid's defiant affirmation. Provincialism and postmodernism are variously hostile or indifferent to all that.

The Poe-Baudelaire axis is a model of an artistic and intellectual phenomenon that travelled well beyond its immediate impetus. Baudelaire's versions of Poe exercised a vast presence in the work of the Franco-Belgian Symbolists, which in turn offered vital ingredients to the modern movement, not least as regards surrealism. Baudelaire excised the name of Poe's Scottish-born stepfather, John Allan, to rebrand him as Edgar Poe; this was a gesture of solidarity as Baudelaire, too, suffered from an oppressive stepfather. The culmination of the French 'Aidgarpo' movement came with Debussy's late, unfinished opera *La Chute de la maison Usher*, but its resonances persisted.

As it continues to cease to be 'almost afraid / To know itself', Scotland still has the potential to match such sophistication. We have writers who demonstrate a hang-up-free, unselfconscious Scottishness that sets no boundaries, whether of space or time. As for a brilliant put-down of the pseudo-sophisticates, the architect Berthold Lubetkin described postmodernism as 'the mumbo-jumbo of a hit-or-miss society'. Artists are of course entitled to pursue postmodernism if that's what they want, but it helps if they can go through modernism first.

Index of Names

HOG'S BACK